Non-Duality

The Groundless Openness

Non-Duality

The Groundless Openness

Douwe Tiemersma

MANTRA BOOKS

Winchester, UK
Washington, USA

First published by Mantra Books, 2012
Mantra Books is an imprint of John Hunt Publishing Ltd., Laurel House, Station Approach,
Alresford, Hants, SO24 9JH, UK
office1@jhpbooks.net
www.johnhuntpublishing.com
www.mantra-books.net

For distributor details and how to order please visit the 'Ordering' section on our website.

ISBN: 978 1 78099 289 1

A CIP catalogue record for this book is available from the British Library.

Translated by Ellen and John Trezevant

Design: Stuart Davies

Printed and bound by CPI Group (UK) Ltd, Croydon, CR0 4YY

CONTENTS

Foreword

What is non-duality? The word appears with increasing frequency in conversations and texts. It refers to a being-experience in which nothing is separated from yourself. This experience arises very easily when you relax. Then the separations between yourself and other things and other people disappear. Everyone seems to know these experiences. It can be a vague understanding, or it can be a clear vision of the truth without duality. In Advaita Vedanta, the current of Indian thought that goes back to the ancient Upanishads of the 8th–6th century BC, the non-dualistic (a-dvaita) vision is elaborated into a philosophy. This non-dualistic vision is present as the highest truth in Buddhism, Taoism and also in Jewish, Christian and Islamic mysticism. Non-duality forms the essence of every spiritual and mystical truth.

The texts in this book refer to the non-dual experience and show the diverse aspects of non-duality in order to give its recognition a better chance. The book is comprised of spontaneous introductions and discussions with people who sought insight into non-duality by asking for descriptions or explanations. These were collected from meetings which were held from the early 1980s onwards. Recordings were made of many of these meetings, some of which were then partially transcribed. Such texts form the most important material of this book. A few other kinds of texts are also included: short pieces of poetry, articles and notes taken by a participant in some of the talks.

Non-duality and openness (the words non-duality, advaita and openness are used interchangeably) are groundless. They cannot be described in positive terms because the separations that the words create are themselves transcended. Also, the words used in this book remain inadequate. They can only give an indication towards awakening. They point towards the being-experience of non-duality and through these references the experience itself can become clearer to the reader. The texts continually connect to your own experience, because it's not about a theory or a system of propositions and ideas. Therefore a loose layout has been chosen for this book with different sorts of texts. Through the continual reference to your own personal experience a clarification can arise. Nevertheless, this explanation forms a more or less coherent philosophy. To a certain extent it's useful to put this philosophy into words, in other words to clarify and supplement the being-understanding.

In your own being-experience a conscious recognition can take place of the undivided openness. These texts refer to that in the most direct manner possible. Through an ongoing orientation to this open essence of yourself and everything, the liberating realization can break through that this groundless openness is *the* truth. It's about a 'direct path'. Therefore it's not necessary to read the book from cover to cover, but rather to linger a bit with shorter pieces of text. Sometimes it's more valuable to remain quietly with one sentence rather than continuing to read on. One thought may be sufficient for the opening of being-awareness.

The realization of non-duality has practical consequences for living and coexisting. All internal and external conflicts arise through divisions. As these separations fall away there is a wholeness without problems.

The texts are arranged in a sequence that is appropriate to the subject matter. After an initial introduction to non-duality, there is a further orientation using autobiographical material which can serve to stimulate the recognition of non-duality in the reader. The third chapter illustrates the diversity of situations in which people find themselves and the high value they ascribe to non-dual openness. From the 'highest' there appears to be a non-duality for all situations. Three types of non-duality then are offered. There is a description of the groundless openness when it is experienced as external (Chapter 4), as well as when it is recognized internally as the deepest core of self-being (Chapter 5). Both perspectives appear to be not different from one another. Thus, there is a non-duality of the groundless openness on the subjective as well as objective side. This third type of non-duality is that of the absolute openness and the relative world. It requires a separate treatment (Chapter 6). The last chapter deals with the nature of the experience of non-duality.

From the available material of introductory talks and discussions only those texts which point directly to the core were selected. So all kinds of themes are left out, such as 'the path' with its difficulties and the traditions with their texts. They are covered in other publications. Also, the selected texts contain a mutual overlap but that is inevitable and even helpful for the recognition to occur within the reader. In their diversity the collected texts offer an insight into all the important aspects of non-duality.

This book is created from the ongoing impulse to express in words that which has yet to be formulated. It's about what is experienced as the most important: freedom and unity, the non-dual openness. It is always already present in everyone as their own source and foundation, but in daily life it seldom receives a clear place in consciousness, in language and in the individual way of life. This book can contribute to a clearer recognition.

There has been a lot of help in creating this book. Thanks go to those who made the recordings and typed out the texts, especially Odile and Willem, and to Wanda who put the texts in order. Thanks to Pia for reading through the text and to Sabine for correcting the manuscript. I am especially grateful to Ellen and John who undertook the huge task of translating the text carefully and effectively into the English language.

1

An initial indication of non-dual openness

Non-duality is simple. When there is relaxation and a clear consciousness, the simplicity is easy to confirm.

Everything is there as light,
light that knows no boundaries;
therefore there is no shadow,
no trace in the transparency;
only a play of light.
You are, I am, that light,
Light that has its center everywhere;
universally we radiate from inside out
unlimited, the wealth
of the light-play,
as long as it continues.

1.1 Openness

1994

Openness is accepting what announces itself in life, without defense and without violence; it is being open in love and compassion, without self-interest and without bias; it is limitless and centerless unity, within which forms are not restricted: *an infinite being.*

Openness is the being-knowledge that This is it: *an infinite being-awareness*; it is your own undivided, and centerless sphere of insight into the indivisibility, a clear being experience that there is no two-ness between yourself and other people or things.

Openness is *the complete happiness-being* in the universal being and consciousness without separations. An all-penetrating joy in and through forms, and also without forms.

Openness is letting all this go, even the last qualities, in pure surrender.

The path to Openness is direct, because Openness is your original and most authentic way of being. It's about a vital and complete awakening of your own true nature and this recognition arises by itself without means. The Openness manifests itself spontaneously when you let go of your ideas about yourself and release your identifications, when you let yourself fully relax in clarity. A radical self-inquiry, possibly combined with yoga and meditation, can be a good preparation.

1.2 Bodily non-duality

Introduction in Gouda, May 12, 2006

What is advaita?

We begin at the beginning, which is inevitable for everyone, even for people who consider themselves to be well advanced, because it's always about the beginning. That beginning is non-duality, the absence of two-ness. The Sanskrit word is advaita. Advaita – 'a' is absence and 'dvaita' from which our words dual (two) and divide (separation) derive – was already a central theme in the ancient Indian Upanishads (8th century BC). In the Upanishads non-duality was seen as the origin of everything. From it arose the splits and divisions that led to the multiform cosmos and the separation between self-being and other. Nevertheless, non-duality remains as the foundation of all.

This can be recognized. You can have a sense that you are so spacious that other people and other things coincide with yourself, that there is a universal non-duality as the essence of both yourself and the universe. In the Upanishads it is expressed as Âtman (the individual self-being) and is identical with

Brahman (the foundation of the world).

The body is a whole

In order to recognize it more clearly, we start with a simple examination of your own body.

When you look at your body, there is usually a duality. Look at your hand and become aware of your situation. Then there is a division between myself and the hand. The hand is an object, a thing that I see. "I see my hand." In this statement 'I' is the subject and 'my hand' the direct object. With this approach I can, for example, take a splinter from my hand. There is a separation between myself and the hand and between the various parts of the hand.

But now go within and experience your hand. Try feeling your hand, while you keep your eyes closed. See how your hand feels from the inside-out. Search for internal divisions... Are there separations?

Someone: Yes and no.

Then where is the separation?

With the skin.

Okay, but, first inside the skin of your hand, is there a separation there? Try looking inside the skin to see, internally, in your own self-sphere.

I experience different places there.

Yes, you can certainly distinguish those. But is there a real separation? A gap?

Yes, I meant that actually, when I said "yes and no". I experience individuality and different places. They also flow into one another.

Is there a real gap?

No, from head to foot, I experience the body as one whole.

What sort of a whole is that? Why are you then one whole? Because there, you are yourself. That is your life, in it you are yourself. So, in that life, in your bodily self-being, there is no separation. This is an extremely important confirmation. If in your bodily living-sphere there is no separation, because it is a unity, even though you can make distinctions within it, then there is no real separation between one part and another part. Seen biologically: in an organism, all parts share with one another. If one part is sick, the whole body suffers. Internally, you can confirm that, in your own feeling body. It is important to recognize: life is one sphere of self-being and within it there are no separations.

The infinite self-sphere

Does your living-sphere stop at the skin? Are you trapped inside the epidermis? From inside-out, do you experience your skin as a border? Is there a border? Take a look. Begin once again with the inner experience of your body and let your attention go to the right. You have learned: somewhere there is a skin, it holds my body in and the outside world begins there. As you internally examine your physical self-being, you notice that the image of your body with its skin is a representation in your thought.

You can now agree to let go of that thought, then you can rely on your own experience, not on what you know. Go then with your attention once again to the right into the sphere of your bodily-feeling self-being. Then go even further to the right. How far to the right can you go without feeling that sphere of the bodily self-being fall away? Stay practical and soberly experience: the sphere of your feeling self-being. Don't make a cognitive picture of your body, but rather, go with your feeling sense further to the right. How far can you go? Where is a border? Then go to the left in the same way. How far can you go? Then go with your attention forwards and backwards, above and below. How is it now? Can you also confirm that your own bodily sphere is infinite, as big as the entire cosmos? Is there anyone who still experiences borders? Apparently not. I haven't encountered anyone yet who still experiences them.

Thus that self-sphere appears to be infinite space, as you see very definitively and clearly how it is from within. You don't use your acquired cognitive knowledge but you really experience how it is. You explore your own sphere experientially, experimentally. You go to the right, to the left, forwards, backwards, above, below.

Then you confirm that there are no real separations in your bodily self-sphere. In the entire cosmos there is not one real separation to be found. It is one cosmos of being-self-being. Experience that very clearly, just as you experience your bodily feeling. In that sphere there is no border, no separation, no duality to be found.

The things of the world

In the universal being-self-being, all material things can arise, all sorts of things that you experience with your senses. But how do they appear? They appear within that sphere of universal self-being. They appear in the sphere in which there are no separations. So the things that appear are not different from yourself. They are yourself, in the same way as your hands and your feet belong to your self-sphere. As you experience that your bodily sphere is infinite, is cosmic, things arise within it. They occupy a certain place without causing a separation anywhere. There remains a sphere of undivided self-being. It is your own sphere in which everything is absorbed. So, there is nothing 'other' that remains. The 'other' people who are there are not really others, because they are absorbed in your own self-sphere. Their self-being is also your self-being. See then that all kinds of conflicts between people no longer arise. When the other is recognized in the sphere of self-being, an incredible amount of problems disappear automatically.

The practical confirmation of the natural situation

Try very practically to confirm what there is to confirm. Then it will also be affirmed: there is no limit to your self-being. That's how it is. From out of your own being-experience it's abundantly clear. Then there is no separation anymore. Then there will be no real conflict anymore. It means an endless relaxation. In returning to the experience of your own sphere, all otherness disappears. Therefore an infinite relaxation arises.

You experience this very practically: all dualities come from the primary duality which arises when you set yourself up at a distance and forcefully keep the others at a distance. All other dualities are secondary. Non-duality is the basis. It is the origin. Separation only comes secondarily.

You see how practical it can be. You can experience it for yourself very precisely: from a limited feeling, you can expand universally, and that is the outflow of love. Within that, everything is lovingly included as yourself. You confirm that it's totally unnecessary to return to making borders between "I am this" and "others are that". When there is just a little relaxation the unity is once again abundantly clear. Apparently the unity is a natural situation. You have to organize everything quite artificially, this in this box, that in that box, in order to separate things out again. That takes effort; it's artificial. As the tension and artificiality fall away, there is relaxation and unity. That's the natural situation.

Because you have seen this very clearly, you say, "No one can fool me any more: I am as large as the cosmos and there is no duality."

Over the border of existence
and back, deep in the center
the freedom
is so clear.

Existence blossoms
like a fountain
of infinite joy.

1.3 A few questions about advaita

From an interview in Ayurveda Actueel 2005

Douwe, how would you explain in a simple way what advaita means to a 10-year-old child?

Advaita means non-duality, the sphere in which there are no separations. You can make this clear to a child by comparing the situation in which someone sees him as an object or attacks him to the complete trust he feels when he is with his mother. In that sphere there is hardly any or even no separation.

The ultimate relaxation in advaita: non-duality. How would you describe that?

When it's about a full and total surrender of everything that is held tightly as an 'I', then relaxation is crucial. Then there is a relaxation that truly goes beyond bodily and mental relaxation. That continues through to the deepest essence of self-being, to the free-being where nothing more of self-being is retained. So then the ego is fundamentally released.

Is the relaxation everything?

Yes, the ultimate, total surrender is relaxation. But, on the advaita-path insight is also crucial, so it's not just about relaxation, but along with it an insight into what reality is: a-dvaita. With a complete relaxation everyone easily slips into a dreamless sleep, without learning anything from it. The insight element gives it a sustained realization.

You hear some people say, "For me advaita is far too woolly and vague."

The direction that is indicated in Advaita has to do with your own practical experience. There's nothing woolly about it. Practical experiences are indicated that everyone knows, for example an experience of deep relaxation or a situation of being wonderfully free in nature, or awakening from a deep blank sleep. Everyone can make the most important observation: "There is a distinct sphere without separations that I value very much."

There are all sorts of circumstances in the world that are continually changing with their correspondingly changing points of view. Couldn't you call that vague?

Most people are not clearly aware of their own situation, even though it changes and fluctuates in all different kinds of ways. They run after a variety of different ideas and want everything. They are defined by vague and changeable ideas and concepts, which color their own experience. Now this is important, then again that, without having a clear perspective of what's really important. Sure, you can call that vague. Really, it's about becoming very sober and confirming everything as clearly as possible.

What is a satsang?

It's a gathering, a being together in the truth that is clearly confirmed and acknowledged. Partly, it's a discussion and an activity on the mental level: all kinds of arguments show that non-duality forms the ultimate basis of everything. And further, there is also a very direct internal functioning of Openness. In that sphere the situation is optimal for surrender, that is, to allow the breakthrough towards realization to occur.

What is there left to say so that this story of each person can dissolve and yet is simultaneously allowed to be?

The core of advaita is that there is nothing to sever. That applies to words as well as to this interview.

Nisargadatta said: "With absolute difference there is no experience. With absolute unity there also is no experience."

As long as there is life, there is the non-duality of experience and the absolute.

air and water commingle
on the shining horizon
the distance disappears
into itself

I see it and
the seeing is infinitely absorbed, I
disappear as distance
from myself

returning
in body and dream
in the darkened morass I
sink endlessly
into myself

in the empty self-being words
rise up
they write
works and
fade
by themselves

1.4 Nothing needs to happen

Bruges, September 28, 2003 and March 30, 2008; notes of the talks taken by a participant

Nothing needs to happen. When you let everything go everything happens by itself. There is no separation between yourself and the tree, between you and the one sitting next to you. Stay quiet in yourself, relax, then every separation disappears. There are no limiting forms. This is a clear being-experience.

You want to change all and everything. You bring on separations. There is a field of tension between you and the other. This creates tension in yourself and causes suffering. Bring your attention back from external things to yourself and then let your attention expand. Stay quietly within yourself with an open awareness.

The lifting of suffering happens by releasing all separations. Your identification with your 'I'-person who feels pain disappears; therefore there is no more tension. The pain may still remain, but it hangs there somewhere off to the side. The pain is absorbed in the greater whole. It doesn't affect you. The pain is simply there.

The dreamless sleep is blank. Time disappears. There is a sphere of self-being without objects.

Stay alert. Be yourself, formless. Return to your sphere of formless being-awareness. Within it everything opens up and is allowed to be. There are no restrictions any longer; there are no more divisions. You are everything. The forms are not different from yourself. Everything remains totally open and light. There are no boundaries.

Life streams on spontaneously. Stay with yourself. Just let everything happen, including your actions. You are not someone who does anything. You are formless. You don't identify yourself with anything. You let everything go. Abandon all control. Surrender yourself. In the total surrender you are everything and everyone. Then everything that continues, continues spontaneously. Everything becomes clear and self-evident. It creates lightness, enlightenment.

Let everything go. That's not doing something; relaxation is doing nothing. When the relaxation stops there is an apparent attachment or blockage somewhere such as fear. Stay in the direct experience of relaxation and expansion. Then the tension will continue to dissolve, because it receives more space. The tension can only continue to exist if you continue to feed it.

Let the fear in and give it space, then it dissolves. The tension can be physical, but also psychological. It can be stubborn to break. Let it in. Allow it to be there in the space. This permission in your open aware being is critical. Conditions, like music, can help to release the tension, but you already are the original source without tension.

Return to yourself. The essential thing is to release and remain alert. All divisions are dissolved. Then you are one. This is what is called the mystical unity. Everything is open. There is no notion of an 'I'. All 'I' constructs are dissolved.

The central issue is to let go of everything. Then all fear of death disappears. Then life is one great play, one great wealth. Openness, release, space, clarity: experience it yourself.

All religious and spiritual currents that give you more space are therefore valuable. To the extent that they work restrictively, you will need to release them. Direct yourself to more space. Remain so until you become completely open.

It can be that there is not complete openness. When you get stuck, take a look to see where you can't move. Throw some light onto your hindrances, obstacles, fears. Determine their structure; recognize the mechanism. Look clearly, then you can see how the situation is constructed. This also means that you become aware once again of the greater space.

Give space to the stuck energies. Absorb the fear within the larger whole. Let yourself completely dissolve and release everything in space yet retain your lucidity. When you stay alert within yourself, everything else becomes clear. In principle you know that. As long as you let the knowing do its work, everything continues by itself.

Stay in the open sphere. Be completely open. Then there is more lucidity and everything becomes clear.

Stay with yourself. Focus yourself steadily inwards on the essential: the core of your being. Relax in your own center. Then everything opens and problems solve themselves. Nothing needs to happen. Everything continues by itself in a good way.

Hear the sound of the church bells. In that experience, you can concentrate on the sound or you can simply remain open. With concentration there is a focus on the external world, which entails a condition of duality. When you are open, the duality disappears and there is just the sound of the bells. In relaxation and openness all distances disappear, you are everything. You hear the sound of the bells, then you are that sound. When you look at someone, you coincide with the other because there is no distance any longer.

Let everything open up. This breaking open gives openness to everything and everyone. It is a total acceptance of everything and everyone. So everything and everyone becomes free, free from the ego's grip. Every expectation that you have with respect to the other restricts them, because then they are not free. Even when you have the best in mind for someone, you limit that person.

Give the other total freedom in all aspects. Only then can they be themselves. The other has the right to be released. That also means that you have become free of your hold on them. Let the boundary between yourself and the other go. In the release of boundaries you become free. Love means releasing the other in the openness of yourself.

Let it deeply penetrate that you're free from all patterns and restrictions. By nature you are completely free. You experience limitations; understand that you're more spacious and don't hold yourself down to restrictions. Be aware of the open atmosphere as your own.

When there are no more boundaries between yourself and others, there can be no more war. War is always about borders, but when all borders disappear, war disappears along with it. By coming into the open, the other is lovingly accepted. In the openness of yourself, everything is allowed to be, everything is accepted. Precisely because it is open, more is possible than ever before. There are many more unexpected opportunities.

The lifting of suffering is not the lifting of desire, but rather the lifting of limiting desire. Don't desire too little. Your desire is endless. When you go along with your infinite desire, you understand your own infinity and so the fundamental suffering is lifted.

Let the relaxation continue on all levels until everything has been completely worked through. Let the relaxation continue radically on all levels. Be careful not to get stuck once again in particular forms. Then the relaxation continues through to complete freedom.

just
a tidal wave of joy
with the bumblebees on the thistle bulb
an ocean of happiness

1.5 What is non-duality (advaita)?

A short introduction, 2000

The Sanskrit word advaita means 'the absence of two-ness' or 'non-duality' (a-dvaita). People can realize that the highest reality of their own self-being and the foundation of the world and the cosmos are identical. Self, others and the world are present in a sphere without separations. In order to indicate this inexpressible sphere the word advaita is preferred over the word 'oneness', which might then indicate that it could be pointed to and therefore be opposed to 'plurality'.

In *experience,* that which you experience is not different from you who experiences it. Every experience is also self-experience, being-experience. You are pure being-consciousness-bliss which coincides with everything and everyone in the Inexpressible.

As *vision,* non-duality is a human and worldview. Within it the boundaries and separations between me and the other, body and mind, micro- and macrocosm, subject and object, man and God are understood to be acquired and relative. This non-dualistic vision is philosophically elaborated in Advaita Vedanta, the Indian tradition which originates from the Upanishads of the 8th–6th century BC. In other traditions, such as Buddhism,

Taoism, Jewish and Christian mysticism and Sufism, the non-dualistic vision is also present as the highest truth.

In *practice,* through daily life, the creating of separations is the cause of many problems, in both the individual as well as collective situation. Conflicts always arise when the one is positioned in contrast to the other, when one person comes to stand against the other. Separation is the source of all conflicts. Then the solution to these problems lies in making the separations radically relative, and in the being-experience of a greater whole in which everything and everyone are included. In that whole the differences persist, but they do not destroy the unity.

Is there a *path* to non-duality? Non-duality appears to be always already present as the most essential core of everything and everyone. Everyone experiences and knows himself in a direct manner, without mediation. There is no distance between yourself and your own essence. Thus, there is no path to non-duality. Starting from a dualistic position some conditions prove themselves to be useful for becoming less stuck in the old identity and structures so as to become more open to non-duality. The most important of these conditions are a clear, open and reflexive attention, a deep relaxation and the nearness of 'someone' in whom non-duality is clearly experienced. For the first two, a well-oriented yoga and meditation practice can be helpful.

aimlessly wandering
through inconspicuous streets
I become entwined with the
glistening houses and wary people
see myself from the bright windows
and the lighted eye,
uprooted, scattered, and vaporized
I am
one with

the emptiness which
supports

1.6 What is enlightenment?

Answers to questions from InZicht [Insight] Magazine (Vol. 7, Number 3, September 2005)

Everyone has a notion of enlightenment. For people who follow a spiritual path, the awareness of that notion increases. Some want to know as precisely as possible where the path leads.

What is enlightenment?

Is there anything to be said about enlightenment? Only in a negative sense. Enlightenment is the being-experience as well as the reality of the falling away of all separations. With what is called enlightenment separations disappear and with them the conflicts and endless running in circles. Above all it has to do with the disappearance of the separations between 'myself' and everything that is experienced as not my own: other people and things, the world, and the cosmos. This dual structure is accepted as fundamental to human existence – notice the grammar of such sentences as "I see that" – but now this duality dissolves. With this melting-together everything which was at first considered as myself becomes a part of the greater whole, while everything in that whole takes on an aspect of self-being. Then self-being and other-being are not different any more. There is no separation any more in the form, quality and location of self-being.

On the path there can also be the experience that your self-being is principally consciousness and that you as being-awareness release the things with which you were formerly identified. That concerns not only the body and the mind, but also the 'I'-world and 'I'-cosmos and ultimately the 'I am consciousness' and the 'I am'. Then there is a sense of 'Nothing'.

As long as there is something, there is the being-experience of the coincidence of Nothing and All. As long as 'All' is, there is the feeling-acceptance of everything in yourself. That is love.

The difficulty of saying anything about enlightenment

The first difficulty in answering the question about enlightenment lies in the fact that understanding always takes place within a framework. Whatever people experience or hear, they understand in accordance with their own situation and their already acquired knowledge. With experiential knowledge this is very clear. If someone says he has eaten a delicious salted herring, you know approximately what sort of experience he has had only if you have eaten such a herring yourself. If you've never eaten a salted herring (only the Japanese and Dutch eat raw fish), it's impossible to discern what you might experience from it. Therefore, to be able to understand any experience your own situation is decisive. The less similarity there is in experience, the more difficult it is to get someone else to understand an experience using words. When it comes to 'enlightenment', it's impossible to make it clear to someone who has no being-experience of enlightenment and who lives exclusively in a dualistic world. Anyone who is not enlightened then also can't recognize enlightenment. He or she only sees what the dualistic perspective makes possible to see: a person. The recognition which originates from beyond the duality falls outside of his or her reality.

A second difficulty lies in the nature of enlightenment itself. In enlightenment the polarity of all oppositions merge into one another, although contrasts may still be used in order to define or specify something. The enlightened 'state' is not something you can point to; it's "not this, not that". About the enlightened 'state', in principle, you can't say anything. It's not to be understood. "If you think you have understood it, you have not understood It" (Kena Upanishad 2.3). Therefore, only negative terms can be given as references to navigate out of the duality or borderline situations where the limits of duality are exceeded. Consider, therefore, that everything said here about enlightenment is referential only and so not a description.

Is it really possible to attain enlightenment?

Enlightenment can never be a positive point, because then it would have a place in duality. You can't go to it, because then it would be at the end of a road in the world of duality. You cannot achieve it, and you cannot grasp it, because 'you' disappear. A person can never achieve enlightenment or realization, because enlightenment is precisely the falling away of that person. Nevertheless there is a being-experience of it, though ultimately it can't be described in positive terms.

Is enlightenment an experience?

When all separations fall away, it's an event that takes place within the individual being-sphere. It's something that happens with yourself. Internally then, there is a being-experience of it, even though the individual being is going to coincide with the being of everything and there is no limiting "I-experience" anymore. It's about a being-experience of self-being which dissolves, a being that is experienced internally. The knowledge and the self-being converge within it. Everyone is themselves, in the purest sense. "It is known as Self" (Kena Upanishad 2.4). The aware recognition is possible. Take a look sometime at the internal experience of your own body that you experience and are from the inside-out. That feeling being-experience is easily unlimited from the inside-out. Take a look. Sometimes you are also aware of your own emptiness in which there are no forms anymore, such as in the deep dreamless sleep, or in the still pauses between two thoughts, or in real happiness. Indeed, reliable being-experience and knowledge of the enlightened 'state' is possible, even though there is nothing to say about it.

There are countless being-experiences that have something to do with enlightenment and which everyone certainly knows, such as a deep relaxation and unity with nature. Then it's about an approach to enlightenment in order to get something definitive from the dualistic position. The words point in that direction. They point towards certain being-experiences which may be relevant to the further development of awareness.

Is it a sudden event? Are there different stages of enlightenment?
Most people have had certain enlightening experiences. On the spiritual path, people become more aware of these experiences and they see more and more clearly into its core. It's a gradual process. Jean Klein called it: preparation of the soil. The "I know what it is" also belongs to this phase.

The crucial element of realization of the individual self-being, of the highest truth, is the real and definitive falling away of the limiting 'I' in a clear and aware manner without a trace of doubt. This falling away and becoming aware is a process whose outcome is no longer in time. It's there instantaneously.

What the value of the enlightened experience and realization is will become evident in time. There is no meaningful way to speak about it in advance. As long as life continues there are countless situations which must reveal how it is. If the realization appears to be stable and seems to be complete, then you can speak about enlightenment.

The 'I'-self has many aspects or levels. The realization of the highest self doesn't necessarily mean that the self-being is non-dual in all its aspects. The opening is certainly definitive, but doesn't always take place directly and completely on all levels. Just think about the various chakra-energies of the many people who appear or appeared to be illuminated, which are or were not always pure. Consider the subtle, rarefied levels on which limiting tendencies or trends (*vâsanas*) may still operate and their effects may still be expressed on the coarser levels in feelings and actions. Thus, realization has different possibilities. There are differences in 'people' who are defined as enlightened. These differences exist not only in character, which continues more or less as long as life does, but in the degree to which the various levels or aspects have been purified, that is, the extent to which non-duality has become a reality in all areas, in all aspects. When it is so, completely and definitively, it can be said to be a true enlightenment.

Can one work towards enlightenment?

The duality of "I will work on my enlightenment" has nothing to do with enlightenment. 'Enlightenment' then is just a vague sense of 'something' that seems important and desirable, a feeling or a sensory notion. You are focused on it as the final goal of a path. That does not pertain to real enlightenment. However, the notion can be very important for weakening the fixation on worldly things and for promoting a focus and an openness. Through that process an increased awareness begins which then changes the experienced situation. The only thing people can do at this stage is to remain in (relative) openness. Tools such as yoga and meditation (focusing on openness) can be helpful. This open attitude allows the Openness to act. At a certain point it takes over the initiative. From the closedness of an 'I', there is no opening for the Openness.

Is a teacher necessary for enlightenment?

It might be possible for enlightenment to break through without the help of a teacher. However, for virtually everyone, a teacher is necessary. We're speaking then about a worldly situation in which there is someone who experiences the openness in another person in such a way that it reflects back upon him or herself. It is the concrete openness of what is called the teacher that is decisive. Especially when it comes to the most subtle processes in the student, the purity, clarity and radicality of the teacher's openness prove to be of the utmost importance. These operate through into the student.

What about the explosive growth in the number of people that are said to be enlightened?

If there is a man claiming to be enlightened, it doesn't mean a thing. There is no one who can say that he or she is enlightened. What is clear is that in the last decade many breakthroughs towards realization have occurred. Sometimes you might think it is spreading like an epidemic. It's not possible to say whether realization is a more common occurrence than previously. Thinking in terms of time and development is not important. The more important question is: how is it with yourself? That also applies to post realization, if there is not a pure and stable "staying established in Brahman". Realization and enlightenment have to show what they are worth.

Is alleged enlightenment distinguishable from genuine?

Not for someone who himself has no knowledge of enlightenment. The only thing you can do is to question yourself as earnestly and as deeply as possible. Then you're already well on the way in the direction of enlightenment. Then you'll be able to clearly see in a maximum way how open the other really is. There is one criterion that people can use to disqualify so-called 'enlightenment': the presence of selfishness. By definition, selfishness and enlightenment exclude one another. If a teacher shows himself to have selfish tendencies, in whatever sense, you must take your leave. Maybe there is something to learn from him or her, but not something that has to do with enlightenment.

To what extent does enlightenment have an effect on the person?

After enlightenment, there is no 'person' anymore. In its place is true emptiness, no more 'I' and 'I'-location. If there are people who choose to call someone enlightened, they should clearly see if that person has no observable ego, but instead openness. Further, there is little more to be said, other than that the openness will show itself, in feeling and in action. That says nothing about the specific behavior because, for example, an aggressive attitude can be used in teaching. Also, character traits continue to exist as long as there is life. It depends on the degree of purification on the various levels as to how heavily they continue to play a role in the behavior of the 'person'. Vanity, for example, can still continue even though there is no identification any longer due to the realization of one's true nature. In the enlightened state these ego remains are worn off and so are absent. Recognize that in the source of yourself.

Look, the white screen
the letters
there

but
their resistance dissolves and
I stretch into the world of words
lost
and beyond them in white

as white
I notice that
there, letters arise in me
worlds of words
scrolling, passing
in white-me

2

Recognition of openness

Because the passing on of individual experience is an important element of the Advaita teaching, 'autobiographical' texts are appropriate for a further orientation. In this teaching, it's not a biography or a description of the necessary ingredients for the realization of non-duality that's important, but rather the chance to recognize something about your own possibilities. It's always possible to experience non-duality, because there's nothing foreign about it. It's always possible to return to the open dimension without separations, because everyone has that as the core of their self-being and because everyone has and has had experiences that have to do with it.

I see the sea and
the soft distance,
sitting here on the dune.

I am the sea and
in the soft distance
I see myself
sitting there on the dune.

I see the sea and myself sitting on the dune
and I am
soft infinite distance of
seeing and being.

2.1 Returning to the openness: the relevance of Yoga and Vedanta

From: Het antwoordloze waarom. Filosoferen tussen Oost en West [The answerless why. Philosophers between East and West], Agora, Kampen 2001, pp. 159–184

Openness and transcendence in the Netherlands

Many people in the West turn to Eastern cultures because they feel something lacking in their own situation and because they recognize or guess that something in the East could fill this gap. Some people experience this lack in a painful way, which gives rise to a focused search. For others the lack exists in an unconscious way, or as a latent openness within which something from the other culture can germinate. Central to this situation is an existential crossing of your own cultural thresholds and a transcendence to a more spacious sphere of living. For myself as well, there was an intuitive interest in transcending cultural limits, a sensitivity and openness for 'the other' which seemed to have something to do with the individual sphere but which was not yet entirely clear to me. Nevertheless, knowledge of 'the other' was not initially connected with an interest in other cultures, but rather with earlier experiences.

From the earliest periods of my life there were more or less spontaneous experiences of feeling myself dissolve. This happened in kindergarten and primary school while running, always running harder with my face into the sun and disappearing into it, with sitting and looking at the water, with playing in the sandbox until everything disappeared and the grains of sand grew larger and larger until only stillness remained. You can still see that with most children, at least when they are not too stressed by television or computer games. In children, thinking has not yet become such a habit so that it constantly fills their entire consciousness. Adults frequently thought that I didn't have my head screwed on right. The same kind of experience was also there in the religious sphere. As a child I found the old expression "If you but trust in God to guide you" (a Calvinistic hymn title) and the idea of Jesus letting the children come unto him quite powerful.

Lots of adolescent kids have a strong interest in physical achievement. Through pushing the limits of their physical capacities they experience transcendence. The experience is one of going faster, higher, deeper, further and thereby becoming more spacious, releasing your self-limitations. That was the basis of my interest in breathing during my middle school period. This interest was strengthened after reading an article in a magazine about a Scandinavian trainer and his athletes who were brought to a very high level of performance through breathing exercises. I wanted this level of performance in my athletics too, so I went to work on breathing exercises. It soon became apparent, in a very direct way, that the breathing exercises met the need for transcendence to such a degree that the physical performance in sports became less important. Through breathing I could influence my consciousness, sometimes in such a radical way that I lost consciousness of myself as an individual.

From the beginning of middle school I was aware of similar changes in consciousness and could produce them through a certain method of breathing and gazing. Although I was for the most part consumed by the daily worries, this other aspect remained present as a steady undercurrent. Sometimes this expressed itself as a naiveté towards events that others might tend to scorn. This naiveté was partly an intentionally held attitude to counter the normalizing effect of others upon me. In adolescence consciousness accepts a limiting structure far too easily by absorbing the influence of other people, by imitating what is considered to be normal within your own peer group. Despite the problems created by others and artificial posturings, your own state can remain quite open. You needn't deal with the difficult stories and constructed realities of others. Such an aware naiveté means letting go of what others might find important. It also means releasing the past and future to a large degree, remaining in the here and now, partially in a space which precedes language, where everything is not yet organized by the words of others. This orientation towards my own valuable experience of openness also helped to further it and this happily remained so, even in the pressured student years. The following text comes from that time: (from *Naar de Openheid [Towards the Openness]*, Miranda Wassenaar, 1983, p. 35, edition Advaita Center, Leusden 2002, p. 36).

I bathe in the sun
in the waving wind
in the call of the soaring gulls
I feel how it floods
over my head and trunk
over my arms and legs

I breathe and laugh
my resistance dissolves
my body stands wide open
the light and the air
stream through me
the last barrier is broken

the call increases
and the urge is so strong
for a greater life
the wind and the rays
absorb me now
endlessly moving

For many people at the end of the sixties and in the seventies the world suddenly broke open; there was a seeing of the possibility of a much larger existence. There was a general movement which was expressed in many different disciplines. In psychology there was Alexander Lowen (bio-energetics), Abraham Maslow (self-actualization), and Charles Rogers (personal growth). In the social-political field there was: non-violent resistance (Gandhi among others), economics (Schumacher), politics (the young Marx, Mao, etc.), living together (experimental living communities, the Hobbit), ecology (Rachel Carson, The Small Earth), and so on. Books from all these different areas were eagerly read, ideas from all quarters discussed and applied. If the government or any other established authority, such as the university administration, obstructed, then demonstrations followed. I, too, participated extensively in reading, discussing and campaigning. The importance of innovative policy was very clear to me. Yet the possibilities of consciousness and the paths of expansion of being remained the central focus of my interest. An open and self-critical attitude was frequently missing from those involved in the beautiful theoretical discussions as well as in the practice of social and political action. That was also the case with most students. Existential transcendence, grassroots democracy, ecological living, and so forth appeared to thrive only when it was accompanied by thorough self-knowledge. Many resorted to using consciousness-expanding drugs. I went the way of yoga and through that came to India.

Yoga for health and as asceticism

My interest in India arose out of the already described passion for transcending my own limits. I had a hunch that in this regard India could mean a great deal. The importance particularly lay in the focused instruction and teaching on the point of transcendence that could be found within the Indian tradition. At the age of fifteen I read something about yoga for the first time. I was so affected by it that I went to the few bookstores in our provincial town to look for a book about yoga. There was only one available and I bought it right away with my scarce pocket money. It was the book by Waldemar *Jong en gezond door yoga [Young and healthy through yoga]* (De Driehoek, Amsterdam 1957). Rama Polderman wrote in his foreword that the book is one "in which everyone can find a guide for a healthy and happy life." Everyone wants such a life and that is how yoga is still used by most men and women in the West.

The number of books on hatha yoga has gradually become legion and yet most titles and introductions are comparable to that of that first book. The majority of people who begin yoga lessons do it to become more relaxed and increase their vitality. Only a small percentage of these people are interested in the further possibilities that are central to the Indian tradition. There is more to it than being just "young and healthy".

The first meeting with yoga can be impressive. I entered the area with hesitancy and only a vague suspicion of what finally awaited me. The book and the words within it contained a quality of sanctity. Cautiously and absorbing everything, I set myself to it. I did the described exercises as well as I could, but with surrender. In retrospect, this attitude of surrender was decisive for the further course of events. In general, the relationship between your own attitude and what actually happens is of great significance. You can predict the development of people by the way in which they deal with instructions and exercises. You can't control these attitudes very easily; to a large extent they are simply a given. People whose sensitivity and openness are already present can only be thankful for it. Through a non-interfering attention such people continue to develop as if by themselves.

Nowadays it's almost impossible to imagine that in 1960 there was hardly a yoga book to be found. However, I located a second one in the provincial library, in German. Given the excerpts which I made at that time, it must have been the Gheranda Samhita. There were concentration and meditation exercises, many of which I tried. Especially at night, after concentrating for awhile, I'd experience a trance, which is to say that I experienced myself as large as the whole reality, or that everything became empty and still. The everyday life in secondary school continued, but openness for the greatest experiential truths that I had now come to know continued to exist in the background. That was also the case during my study of biology which began in 1963, when I came into contact with the East only now and then. This contact became stronger in the late sixties with yoga lessons in the Kosmos and Paradiso, and especially with yoga teacher training in Baarn.

The yoga that I practiced in this period contained a strong discipline. Its starting point was the physical body and the goal was to transcend it. Due to that tendency, this yoga leaned towards asceticism. An ascetic systematically guards himself from all sorts of things that most people find pleasant and natural, and does things that others might find unpleasant. He wishes to rise above the body and so he tries to minimize the physical needs such as eating, drinking, moving, sexuality. In this formulation, asceticism rightly gives cause for much criticism, especially when you see the extreme forms that it can take. These extreme forms also occur in India for those who want to be totally independent of everything connected with the body. The yogi dedicates himself to no longer eating, no longer drinking, no longer sleeping, no longer breathing, no longer observing, no longer thinking. Through this he follows a special path in the hopes of obtaining magical powers, immortality or liberation from the cycle of rebirth.

In the desire for liberation there is a focus that can be a positive value. The ascetic believes that it is possible to arrive at a freer mode of existence. It is sought in the spiritual realm, in contrast to the material condition. The attention is directed inwards. There is a perception of your own spiritual reality and that means liberation from the domination of the material world.

Although the strong opposition between the spiritual and material – and the strict choice for the spiritual – cannot be defended, nevertheless the West has a lot to learn from the spiritual orientation of India.

The relationship between body and mind

I was deeply struck by the idea in the yoga tradition that the physical situation is a basis for spiritual development. It's about the lifting of physical obstacles in order to assist in spiritual development. Vitalization and purification of the body through postures and breathing exercises can change your entire way of being in a positive manner. In *Voorbij het bewuste. Dagboek van een priester-yogi [Beyond the conscious. Diary of a Yogi Priest]* (Ambo, Utrecht 1969, p. 153), one of the first books appearing in the subsequent boom of literature on yoga, Ruud Lohman wrote: "Wouldn't doing three minutes of sarvangasana on your head often be better than one or two hours of professional counseling?" [...] "I know for sure that meditating without padmasana [the lotus position] is a flop more frequently than it is with it." [...] "I also know that a flexible spine helps you to realize that you are a temple for the Holy Spirit and that the Kingdom of God is already within me, waiting for the day when I will put aside the obstacles to its unfolding." Lohman's emphasis on the importance of the body's influence on the mind has always remained with me. The material and energetic-feeling body form a basis for the mental state, and so a sound physical foundation is often very useful for spiritual development.

This and many other issues were also clear in meditation. When you no longer focus on external things in the world but instead turn reflexively towards your own situation, you become aware of the physical, energetic, emotional and mental processes. With an open attention you can see the influences from the environment as well as your reactions to it. Then the conditionings are clearly seen, so they don't dominate any longer and can be released. In short, through meditation you get to know yourself better. Although it's also possible to arrive at a similar subjective truth through contemporary cognitive psychology, the meditative study of the mind is far more direct.

One of the results of meditative self-inquiry is the absence of a separation between body and mind. This is connected with the experience that there is a certain body present, even on the mental level. There is a sliding transformational scale from the hard substance of the body, through to the energetic body, to the mental body and vice versa. The relation between body and mind is unthinkable if a fundamental difference is assumed. From the experience of a sliding scale of energetic structures, the mutual influences of body and mind are no longer a problem. Voluntary movement, for example, becomes visible as a mental pattern, which materializes itself via the feeling-energetic sphere in the body. There is a transition from what is called the subtle body to the coarser, material body. This transition is observable in meditation. My doctoral thesis concluded with a philosophy of the body in this sense (*Body Schema and Body Image. An interdisciplinary and philosophical study*, Swets & Zeitlinger, Lisse/Amsterdam 1989).

The experience of the energetic sphere and the subtle body is hardly taken seriously in the modern West. The notion of energy in Western science is therefore different than the notion of it in Indian traditions. In the West it is abstracted from experience and has become theoretical. It has a place among other things in the thermo-dynamic theory of object processes. In the context of yoga, however, it stays very close to experience and remains connected to the grammatical first person, myself, for example, in daily life when we say: "I don't have any more energy." Energy can develop from out of the physical experience. In India, this knowledge has led to its own science and technology. The transition from an exclusively material experience towards the perception of an energetic experience already indicates a certain kind of liberation. There can also be similar discussions comparing the notions of time and death in both Western and non-Western cultures. I have elaborated on these themes in several articles.

When yoga is practiced in a superficial way for health, with an eye to performance or to get into a trance, the pleasure fades out of it rather quickly. One soon gives up and starts looking for something else. Some people continue further into the health area or the esoteric yoga direction, but in the former you cannot speak about real yoga, and in the latter you are likely to end up roaming endlessly in esoteric circles. Ruud Lohman writes in his aforementioned book about his meeting with a yogi that he named 'FOG', the 'Frustrated Occult Genius': an example not to follow.

The yoga of loving devotion

In the seventies I experienced bhakti yoga, as a loving focus on the divine. It is a deepening of yoga, because within it the focus shifts and expands to a dimension that goes beyond one's own world. I went for a retreat to the monastery of the Ramakrishna Mission at Gretz, near Paris. Here the communal chanting of "Hari Om, hare Krishna..." melted my emotions. I felt both Krishna, the incarnation of Vishnu known from the Bhagavadgîtâ, and Ramakrishna, an enlightened Indian teacher from the 19th century and priest of a Kali temple, to be present as the shining source of love. Surrendering to this love means both a merging with and presence in an atmosphere of light and infinite love. Within it the heavenly song is softly continuing into infinity. There is no notion of being a person any longer, nor of separation. Nothing needs to happen. I had already known that with the image of Jesus, who here is one with Ramakrishna. Students of Ramakrishna often draw parallels with Jesus. They also see Christianity as a way of loving devotion *(bhakti)*. Ultimately, God is Love. Within that love, all forms, including one's own, are absorbed and made relative.

Vivekananda, the main disciple of Ramakrishna, proclaimed the teachings of his master to the world like a Paul figure. After his visits (beginning in 1893) a significant movement resulted in both the United States and Europe. Christopher Isherwood, Aldous Huxley and Gerald Heard were some of the famous people involved in this movement. In the thirties they wrote articles for the magazine *Vedanta and the West*. These were included in the books *Vedanta for the Western World* (Unwin Books, London 1948) and *Vedanta for Modern Man* (Mentor Books, New York 1952), which were eagerly read in the seventies. The word 'Vedanta' refers to the last section of the Vedas (the ancient religious literature of India from around 1200 BC) called the Upanishads. It also refers to the philosophical schools based upon those texts. Because the Upanishads contain a variety of texts there are various schools, but the Vedanta of Ramakrishna, Vivekananda and their followers sought to synthesize the different viewpoints. The loving focus towards God and the broadening of the insight relative to the identity of the self and the absolute go hand in hand. From this point of view, all religions exist merely as so many different pathways towards the realization of God.

Through my contact with Ramakrishna and his form of Vedanta, the change of identity through a loving focus on the divine became clearer to me than ever before. In contrast to the distance between God as the creator and man as his creation in Christianity, here God and man were not so clearly separated. Through inner focus on the divine, you come ever closer to the divine sphere. Ramakrishna stressed: "What you focus on you will become." That is a truth which applies to everyone, everywhere. Images and symbols also play an important role in that, since for me the image of Ramakrishna still remains as a shining light. Through loving focus, the image and sphere of the image became increasingly real. The distance that had existed decreased and disappeared in the merging together with the image in total surrender, through absorption into the divine sphere. This sphere remains present to a greater or lesser degree even in daily life. Thus the world and life are spiritualized and grow in the atmosphere of love in which everyone is absorbed.

Every spiritual path has its own dangers. One danger of the path of devotion that I noticed is the dulling of spiritual passion. When the exuberance of the religious experience weakens, the secondary phenomena come to the fore: instability of the emotions, getting stuck in the beautiful sense of love and togetherness, the intolerance towards other beliefs, rigidity of the external forms. In the external forms of Hinduism there are strong culturally defined phenomena: swamis, sacred formulas, rituals, etc... which caused me to take some distance. The preaching of the similarity of all religions, including that of Vedanta with modern science, was also for me too simplistic. My later teacher Nisargadatta Maharaj, of whom more is spoken below, readily agreed to having Indians and Westerners come in the evenings to sing devotional songs (*bhajans*), because he had promised his own teacher to do so, but he resolutely sent me away. My own path was another. Later, when I came to India for a time and visited the temples of Krishna (Brindavan, Mathura), I was physically sick from the external excesses and limitations, both of the images and the so-called holy people with all their fuss. On the purer mystical path there exists a freedom with respect to images and feelings. Therefore for me, the space of consciousness and the aware insight were decisive.

The yoga of knowledge

Knowing more means being more. To become familiar with a greater space than what has previously existed is to participate in it. Thus knowledge of all areas fascinated me and I sought to synthesize it all in a complete worldview. So I studied biology (with physics, chemistry and geology) and philosophy along with many other areas. When I studied philosophy, I elaborated on the experience of existential increase by writing an article for the magazine *Cimedart,* of the Philosophical Faculty of the University of Amsterdam ("Philosophizing and studying philosophy as a change-of-being", *Cimedart* 4 5 Feb. 1974 and in *Verdwijnende scheidingen [Disappearing Separations],* Advaita Center/Asoka 2005).

At that time, it was not clear that the piece would be included in the faculty newspaper. The editor didn't think that it fit into the academic tradition: a characteristic situation. Only through the intervention of Otto Duintjer was it eventually included in 1974.

The merging of knowledge and being is central to the tradition of Advaita (non-dualistic) Vedanta. Insight into one's own true nature, the unconditioned self-being, allows this Self-being to manifest unhindered. During my philosophy studies I turned to the Advaita literature and wrote a thesis on the great Advaita philosopher Shankara (8th century) and the (deceased in 1995) Jewish philosopher, Levinas. The Infinite which manifests itself in other men (according to Levinas), becomes (with Shankara) especially visible in the teacher, as the Other. But there is a clear difference, which is exemplary in the comparison between the Upanishadic (Vedantic) and Judeo-Christian visions. In the Vedanta the Infinite is present in all beings and all things. It is the source of the World, yet also the core of yourself. The identity of the infinite outside you (*Brahman*) is identical to the infinite within you (*Âtman*). If you return to the heart of yourself as pure consciousness this can be directly confirmed. Levinas' ethics come into play only so long as you think and experience that there is a separation between yourself and the other: the first duty I have is my responsibility towards others. But when unity with the other and everything is realized, the 'I'-other structure and its concurrent sense of responsibility disappear. Then behavior is automatic and without ego-centricity. In practical experience both truths go together, but the central point lies in the sphere of unity.

Towards the end of 1968 Wolter Keers, who had received training in the Advaita Vedanta tradition in India, became editor of the magazine *Yoga Kroniek* (*Yoga Chronicle)*, and soon renamed it *Yoga and Vedanta*. This magazine, which had been colored by a strongly modified Western form of hatha yoga (Rama Polderman) and theosophy (Dra. C. Keus), changed colors and now published the direct and clear Advaita teaching. Many readers were shocked and unhappy. Others, myself included, thought it was great and visited the lectures and discussions of Keers. I felt much more at home with Jean Klein, who was regularly invited by Keers to speak in the Netherlands (Elspeet), and with whom a less Calvinist atmosphere prevailed. Jean Klein came from the tradition of North Indian shaivism (shaivism of Kashmir), where the paths of Advaita and energetic yoga are combined. Both the energetic exercises and the advaita talks supported the development of the insight of being free from every limiting identity. It concerned insight into the highest Self (*paramâtman*), insight into the individual identity without name and form, that is, seeing through the artificiality and relativity of your own identity in the worldly situation and the recognition of your own true nature. When you realize this, the sphere of the highest self becomes reality, and that is liberation (*moksha*). Here knowledge and being come together.

Traditionally, the presence of a teacher is seen as a requirement for this breakthrough. This teacher himself should have the highest insight, should be liberated. In India, such teachers have a social standing as models of the liberated state in word and deed. I have Wolter Keers to thank because through him, in the late seventies, I came into contact with the one who would become my teacher. Wolter introduced me to the book *I Am That, Talks with Nisargadatta Maharaj* (Chetana, Bombay 1973, etc.).

The teacher and liberation

How do you know that you have found an authentic teacher, the teacher for you? The conviction can grow through a long-term contact, if you increasingly resonate with the meaning of his or her words, with the core of the teacher himself. In my case it was a sudden happening. The contents of *I Am That* hit me like a bomb. The truth of Advaita had never come over me so directly and so clearly. Also, that the teacher was still alive was an incredible piece of luck. I knew right away: I must go to him. If there was anyone existing in the world to whom I must be a student, it was Nisargadatta Maharaj. I marveled in the inner knowledge that the reality behind the printed words of *I Am That* was the ultimate truth, that this reality is fully present in and around the teacher and that this reality would fully manifest itself to me in his presence.

Thus, I had to go to Bombay, but my work and family circumstances prevented a premature departure. But look, a miracle happened: within a short period of time the obstacles disappeared, bit by bit, like the lifting of a fog. When it is time for you, the necessary conditions come as if by themselves. It was the same for me. I went to Bombay in late 1979 like a moth to the flame. That's how it felt. Without having ever been in the East, I stood one day, suitcase in hand, on a hellishly busy street in downtown Bombay. Inundated by the bombardment of impressions, I stood looking at the swarming, noisy life of poverty, disease and death. I listened to the cacophony of the dying, screaming, bells ringing, singing, and took in the smell of rotting waste, incense, gasoline and flower garlands. I let it happen. Later, when all kinds of personal plans in the city were in tatters through the chaos and inimitable spirit of the Indians, I understood that you have to let go of everything and you have to go into the maelstrom of Maya, the play of appearances. If you try to hold onto your Western ideas of efficiency and order, you'll go crazy.

I hardly knew where I was supposed to be in the city center

other than: "opposite a public urinal." In the house of Nisargadatta Maharaj you can smell it very clearly. Later, when someone asked him why he burned so many incense sticks, he said: "To cover the stench of urine." Nevertheless, for all the times that I came to the loft the smell never created a nuisance, not any more than the intense noise of the street below. We were focused on other things. Later, when I heard a cassette tape of a conversation with Maharaj, I was surprised by the noise. Others asked how was it possible to communicate normally. Thus, spirituality is not dependent on circumstances. Similarly, the teacher does not depend upon externals. Many visitors saw nothing in the old man who sat on a chair, smoking and was often half screaming with offensive speech. However, if you looked closely, there was the purest spirit of truth and love. That someone had to translate Marathi, the regional language, into English was also not a difficulty. When you are focused on the meaning, the form in which it's expressed is either transparent or doesn't exist at all. The significance crystallizes by itself and becomes a reality without interference. That is the 'direct path' which you don't plan, but instead just cross.

"Why did you come you here?" was the stern question from the toothless old man on the low loft. I replied that I had to come and that I had had enough of the world of concepts. I saw him nod and heard him mutter that this was a good start. Sitting on the floor in a corner I just let everything happen. Maharaj liked a fierce debate, which by the way he always won. Especially when someone from the academic world had objected to his statements, he would spring up and begin the fight. Within a short period of time the attacker was cut down to size and had to admit that he didn't know what he was talking about. If no one dared to speak, Maharaj challenged us: "Get up and fight!" But those who had been in the loft for a while came to know that as soon as someone's head rose above the cornfield, it came off. It was not only because of this that I said very little in the few weeks that I was there. If you go along to where the words indicate, you're on a real edge where things happen. I was there and not in the world of words. Maharaj seemed to accept this because he only asked me something now and again. But at a given moment he said that I should come separately to him to receive a mantra, to get an initiation. Thereafter the whole process took place very quickly. Regarding this process there follows here below a piece of text from an article that appeared after his death in 1981 ('Sadguru Sri Nisargadatta Maharaj', *Yoga and Vedanta* 23, Number 4 (December 1981), 171–174). It has to do with the three forms in which Maharaj appeared to me. They first appeared in the semi-conscious sphere, but afterwards were the greatest reality.

"The first was a terrifying form: that of a murderer. A murderous force gripped me by the throat and struck me in the heart, the black Durga/Kali with her tusks, and the great demons of Tantric Buddhism. They were my own homemade images, as correlates of fear. Before the face of the Absolute the 'I' jumped and twisted and tried to escape, to survive the suffocating death. But it had no chance as long as it remained in the open situation. The self as witness looked on, as the 'I' literally died and let go. It can only happen this way. At a certain point, in addition to the conscious Self there was still a residue of the personal 'I' remaining at a distance, but annoyingly, with tension. This time Maharaj appeared in the form of a magician. He stood there and let the 'I' disappear, without doing anything. Finally, the last rarefied tension disappeared from the very spacious 'I'-sphere, thanks to Maharaj. But beyond the personal/bodily 'I' there is also the formless 'I-am'; within this there can also be tension. When that disappears, then there is the Absolute in a completely unfettered manner. This transition can be seen as the last phase of the death process of the 'I'. This rarefied 'I' must fall into the abyss of the Absolute. How is that possible? The guru appeared again, now without form, in a wordless knowing that he was the

Absolute and that he would absorb me in love. So the 'I am' consciousness disappeared and with it any separation between consciousness and non-consciousness, between being and non-being, between the 'I' and 'the other'."

About that 'state' there is not much to say, because every structure of knower and known and of language itself disappears. However, there is a 'knowing' of this 'state', a knowing that is not different from conscience and the 'one who knows'. 'The one' who 'knows' is said to be a 'knower' (*jnani*). After such a breakthrough there is nothing. Then there appears a cosmic scale of energy without structure. This remains present, even as the energy is compacted locally in the forms of things in the world. It's worth noting that there is no first person who becomes involved in the forms of the world. The forms remain at a distance, transparent and in a limited area. At a distance everything continues to turn: the traffic, the noise, the talking, but it keeps turning in a free manner, without connecting to your own great reality. It is a huge surprise that there is still a world, that everything continues. How is it possible when everything has dissolved? There is no time and place, and yet a dynamic world and a bodily 'I' still manifest.

In the morning Maharaj saw directly how things were. "It's no longer necessary that you come here," he said. "You can go." Ramesh Balsekar translated and repeated these words because I had displayed no visible reaction. Suddenly internal confusion arose about 'my' situation, because the thought came up: "This is it, but what are the consequences? This is immense, nothing is certain anymore. Am I sufficiently established in the unfathomable?" With the farewell to Maharaj every confusion disappeared. Without words he confirmed the new situation. Then there was only the infinite sphere of being, of being-awareness, bliss-being: the ocean of *sat-cit-ānanda*. At a certain moment I was aware that I was sitting in the sand at Chowpatty Beach.

The meeting with the ultimate teacher (*sadguru*) is the greatest happiness in life that can befall you. That is the teacher who doesn't see himself as a teacher, but who knows himself as Openness and is so known. It is this Openness which provides the necessary space for dissolving the 'I'-residues. It is also the Love that is necessary for the ultimate confidence that everything is good, so that the last tension can fall away. It is also the ultimate confirmation of knowing: This is it. This knowledge is already present and it is a knowing certainty in the wakefulness. The belief and confirmation in what the teacher says removes any remaining doubts. The teacher has a human form but that is needed to build the bridge from the limited to the unlimited. The combination of form and formless make his function possible: the realization (becoming aware as well as the materialization) of Openness within the student, the merging of teacher and student. Many theological issues exist around the figure of Jesus, especially concerning his human and/or divine nature and his mediation. These problems are truly theoretical. If anyone has met Jesus or another teacher as their ultimate teacher *(sadguru)*, it is precisely clear how these two natures coincide.

Integration with the ongoing life

It's miraculous that the world and time return. The indescribable emptiness/fullness continues to exist as reality, but the ecstasy of the first days becomes less strong, the reality of the physical worldly existence returns. The relationship between both realms varies. Sometimes there is just the pure happiness of the one self-being within which everything is included. There is a reluctance to allow the process of world creation to continue. Sometimes the world establishes itself as an independent reality and exerts a strong attractive force. Then there may even be a major involvement in the worldly concerns with all their tensions and an amazement that the process continues. So there were these two spheres of reality existing in a changeable manner. In my professional work the forces were still operating to continue to perform well; at certain periods I proved ready to deal with all the consequences. However, there was no longer a full immersion in the activities. It was clear that, as long as there is a world, there will also be an integration of the two spheres.

This integration of the non-dual with the dual gradually became established. The everyday life of both home and work actively continued. It required attention and, at least in part, worked via the old tendencies. What was principally missing was the basic heaviness of existence and the fog obscuring my own original nature. A lightness came, a clear light, without a person for whom this would have been unbearable. Precisely because of that everything could develop further in a natural way. The integration grew stronger through habituation and a better understanding of phenomena on all levels (sensory, emotional, mental and super-natural). What was initially half-conscious or unconscious now entered increasingly into the light, including the knowledge of causal relationships between phenomena: when this happens, it causes that. Actions have their consequences, and a certain orientation lets a certain reality arise. That's how it works. Without consideration and without choice there was acceptance: let the further purification just happen. The world and its activities seem to continue to exist, but they don't detract from the unity. So not only is the self liberated, but the world is too. For as long as they exist in experience, together they form an indescribable unity.

Advaita Vedanta has a doctrine regarding "liberation in this lifetime" *(jîvanmukta)* which derives from the question, how it is possible that life can continue after liberation? Liberation always means the release from the karmic forces which propel the life of man into the cycle of birth and death. Without karmic identification there would be no more life or death. Shankara used different metaphors to explain the further continuation of life of the liberated: life continues to flow, just as the potter's wheel continues to spin for a time after the pot has been made, or just as an arrow continues forth in its flight, and just as someone with an eye disease continues to see the moon in duplicate for awhile, though he knows his double vision to be an illusion. The impulse which was already active may continue to function after liberation. This is the karma that has already begun to work itself out *(prârabdha karma).* Shankara himself counseled overcoming the remaining karma through a certain discipline. In contrast to the situation of the ignorant, the *prârabdha karma* produces no new karma, because there is no more attachment and no more identification. With the breakthrough of the Insight there is the fundamental liberation from karma; after the physical death there are no more karmic remains to cause a new incarnation.

Indeed, the lives of the great teachers were marked by manners of behavior and speech which were colored by their own personal characteristics. The behavioral modes of Jesus and Buddha were different, as were those of Ramakrishna, Ramana Maharshi and Nisargadatta Maharaj from the Hindu tradition. They all demonstrate that there is a degree of maturation and purification which occurs after the first liberating experience or becoming aware of freedom. After the liberating breakthrough it can take a longer time before the "establishment in Brahman" is complete. Although the most important event has already taken place, this can further stabilize. When the path is condensed by focusing on the highest, there is the chance that you've passed by a number of things along the way that will need to be processed later. Maharaj drove us on with great speed through all the worlds to the Emptiness. Afterwards – since apparently there was an 'afterwards' – blocks of energy still stuck in various areas had to be released and the world accepted in a new way. That's possible, because the 'negative path' towards being-nothing ultimately arrives at being-everything. First there is a return to the origin, pure being-consciousness, but then the world returns, too. This world can remain in the sphere of infinite consciousness (idealism) to the extent that consciousness is the point of view. Also, this being-awareness and the world of phenomena can telescope into one another in the Inexpressible. That's infinite love, in which the self-being-awareness gives itself away. That's how being-nothing goes together with being-everything.

There was, despite all the pain of hesitation and relapse, the continuing experience that duality, the world with all its separations, is included within the non-duality. That duality depends upon a limited perspective and has little significance in relation to the non-duality. The non-duality is inexpressible not only because it is beyond all duality, but also because it includes it. In non-duality nothing is discarded, not even the duality, because then there would be a separation. That is the highest concept in Advaita Vedanta. Those who speak only in positive terms about Advaita as the perfect state neglect this union of duality and unity. Enlightenment is the ultimate, but the highest also exists within the lowest; suffering also exists within delight. Nothing is excluded, precisely because everything is one. This unity is not a positively formulated oneness, and that's the reason why the term 'a-dvaita' (not-two) is more suitable than, for example, 'oneness'. It has to do with an inseparability that cannot be put into words. An answer to the questions of life is not to be found there. The questions have fallen away. They can re-emerge, but then only from the 'standpoint of practical life' *(vyavahâra-avasthâ)* in which people experience themselves as thinking and acting in the world. Advaita Vedanta distinguishes that situation from the situation of the 'standpoint of the highest truth' *(paramârtha-avasthâ)*, where no separations and limitations are present. From this 'position' the names and forms are not real limitations, because the phenomena exist within the one *Âtman-Brahman*. In practice, there is the experience that the other and the world are not different from yourself. That is a state without egocentricity, a state of love.

Then love wells up,

living water
from a source that never restrains
its excess,
because it
has turned inside-out.

2.2 Spiritual experiences

Loneliness, liberation, psychosis

(From the lecture at the Symposium "Psychiatric disorder or spiritual experience? Philosophical views from Zen and Yoga", Rotterdam, December 9, 2004)

Just after the Second World War, when I was two years old, my father was in an accident and had to go to a university hospital far away for treatment. My mother went to visit him, but due to the poor transportation then was gone the entire day. Many days I remained alone in my bed with only a neighbor or an aunt occasionally stopping by to check in on me. I became aware of myself, standing in my bed, feeling that I was very alone. I felt totally abandoned, completely let down. There was a sense of despair, of the inability to exist in the large empty space. Everything flowed together, everything fell away. "I can't do anything anymore" is how it felt. "Everything is lost, everything is gone." Then, when I gave in to it, a wonderful thing happened: everything disappeared and there arose a being-experience that I, myself, was the great emptiness, without form. In this transition there was a great experience of joy.

While growing up, the expanded experience-sphere disappeared partially into the background, but never completely. Most likely it played a part in starting to practice yoga, at a time when hardly anyone else was doing it. Through the practice of yoga and meditation the original state returned quite often. This was particularly the case after strong energetic experiences. Strong energies become released precisely by breaking through the limited individual form in which those energies are contained. You are those energies, so the experience of it is very intense. Later with Nisargadatta Maharaj there was a transition in a very radical manner and with great clarity.

It seems to me that the most important elements or moments of what happened apply to every spiritual path. They are the following:

a) There are special events in a person's early years that lead sooner or later to a spiritual interest and a spiritual path. Often these are traumatic events.
b) These experiences lead towards a situation in which the 'I' experiences an infinitely all-embracing space in which the 'I' can no longer exist: the Nothing. In the border area all the categories of space and time, inside and outside, self and non- self converge. There is a chaos, in which nothing is left to hold onto.
c) Here, fear usually arises, fear for your own existence as an 'I'- person. This fear can continue to build up through increasing tension. It's an existential contraction of the 'I', because it experiences that if the Nothing-space continues to fully manifest, its number is up.
d) With a good spiritual development, sooner or later there is a surrender, which is experienced positively as a leave-taking of the limits and restrictions of the 'I'. It's a liberation, an enlightenment, not an escape but rather an acceptance and thereby freedom in non-duality.

What happens with spiritual development is comparable to the emergence of a psychiatric disorder. Here again the central problem is of unity and separation, of self and non-self, being and not-being. In many cases, the elements a), b) and c) are quite similar. If the surrender d) doesn't occur, and the manifestation of the Nothing continues, the 'I'-anxiety can increase and become a fear-implosion, which is a psychosis. The most important therapy seems to be communicating that you always already are that Nothing and giving your trust to someone who has already realized that himself. But with which psychiatrists is that the case?

Further experiences from childhood

Children are much closer to openness than adults. When adults become more aware of the openness more experiences of it from childhood seem to reappear. Initially, the experiences were spontaneous and natural, even though later they may have become encapsulated by learned patterns.

So I remember light from my childhood as a doorway to an infinite sphere of light: the light that went through an upper window above the toilet and which made a flat shape upon the wall, the light in the baby stroller, running towards the light in the street, viewing sunlight upon the water, or walking on a forest path streamed with light. Wherever the sunlight came in upon me, the separation between myself and that light instantly disappeared. There was a dissolving into the light and then there was only light and nothing else.

Even when just sitting still and looking at things the sense of distance easily disappeared. Then there was no interpretation and no distant 'I'. There was a merging together and becoming one with, for example, the grass of the field and the geranium in the window-box. It also happened while listening to the wind in the trees, and the murmur of the sea.

As children we would go on Sunday afternoon walks with my father. Behind our little village there was a footpath. My father would lead us there to show us how beautiful the plants growing along the side of the path were, the grass too, if you only looked closely enough. Each plant was a miracle. And, suddenly I saw it! The grasses with their blades and flowers were beautiful, and were totally themselves. They let themselves be seen from an infinite depth, like a miracle. The miraculous world was one and I had a part in it. There was a great, infinite unity, without words and thoughts. That reality stayed with me the whole week. I went back there one day with a friend and he too felt that greatness. However, daily life went on and washed over the experience. Thus, later I declined my friend's proposal that we should go back again to revisit the path. Toughness became opposed to vulnerability, the external in contrast to the internal secret and the former got the upper hand. That's often how it goes in life.

These experiences from childhood can return later in the world of experience. They show that familiarity and unity with everything were always already present and that unity was the starting point for the duality which later came to the fore.

Notes on a subsequent experience

It's early morning, and I'm still lying in bed. It's a free day without appointments. It was a wonderful night's rest and I turn over again. But there's no more sleep to come. Only the sphere of sleep remains, a big lazy sphere without thinking and desiring. Passive and without a center, I perceive the light that comes through the window and the sounds in the distance. They have no effect on me, but as qualities are not separate from myself. I and everything are barely differentiated in this sphere of spacious relaxation. Then there is an impulse to give shape and form, a crystallization and hardening of myself, of qualities and of time, the things from yesterday and the day to come. The impulse disappears and once again there is the great field of Origin. As quiet joy and empty being-awareness I am universal. Even later I remain without distance as universal joy and being-awareness, observing the formation of the world, the washing and the breakfast...

2.3 Foreword to *I Am That* by Nisargadatta Maharaj

This is the Foreword to the 1981 edition of I Am That. Talks with Sri Nisargadatta Maharaj, 1981, etc. (Publisher Chetana, Bombay).

That there should be yet another addition of I AM THAT is not surprising, for the sublimity of the words spoken by Sri Nisargadatta Maharaj, their directness and the lucidity with which they refer to the Highest have already made this book a literature of paramount importance. In fact, many regard it as the only book of spiritual teaching really worth studying.

There are various religions and systems of philosophy which claim to endow human life with meaning. But they suffer from certain inherent limitations. They couch into fine-sounding words their traditional beliefs and ideologies, theological or philosophical. Believers, however, discover the limited range of meaning and applicability of these words, sooner or later. They get disillusioned and tend to abandon the systems, in the same way as scientific theories are abandoned when they are called in question by too much contradictory empirical data.

When a system of spiritual interpretation turns out to be unconvincing and not capable of being rationally justified, many people allow themselves to be converted to some other system. After a while, however, they find limitations and contradictions in the other system also. In this unrewarding pursuit of acceptance and rejection what remains for them is only skepticism and agnosticism, leading to a fatuous way of living, engrossed in mere gross utilities of life, just consuming material goods. Sometimes, however, though rarely, skepticism gives rise to an intuition of a basic reality, more fundamental than that of words, religions or philosophic systems. Strangely, it is a positive aspect of skepticism. It was in such a state of skepticism, but also having an intuition of the basic reality, that I happened to read Sri Nisargadatta Maharaj's I AM THAT. I was at once struck by the finality and unassailable certitude of his words. Limited by their very nature though words are, I found the utterances of Maharaj transparent, polished windows, as it were.

No book of spiritual teachings, however, can replace the presence of the teacher himself. Only the words spoken directly to you by the Guru shed their opacity completely. In a Guru's presence the last boundaries drawn by the mind vanish. Sri Nisargadatta Maharaj is indeed such a Guru. He is not a preacher, but he provides precisely those indications which the seeker needs. The reality which emanates from him is inalienable and Absolute. It is authentic. Having experienced the verity of his words in the pages of I AM THAT, and being inspired by it, many from the West have found their way to Maharaj to seek enlightenment.

Maharaj's interpretation of truth is not different from that of Jnana Yoga/Advaita Vedanta. But, he has a way of his own. The multifarious forms around us, says he, are constituted of the five elements. They are transient, and in a state of perpetual flux. Also they are governed by the law of causation. All this applies to the body and the mind also, both of which are transient and subject to birth and death. We know that only by means of the bodily senses and the mind can the world be known. As in the Kantian view, it is a correlate of the human knowing subject, and, therefore, has the fundamental structure of our way of knowing. This means that time, space and causality are not 'objective', or extraneous entities, but mental categories in which everything is molded. The existence and form of all things depend upon the mind. Cognition is a mental product. And the world as seen from the mind is a subjective and private world, which changes continuously in accordance with the restlessness of the mind itself.

In opposition to the restless mind, with its limited categories – intentionality, subjectivity, duality etc. – stands supreme the limitless sense of 'I am'. The only thing I can be sure about is that 'I am'; not as a thinking 'I am' in the Cartesian sense, but without any predicates. Again and again Maharaj draws our attention to this basic fact in order to make us realize our 'I am-ness' and thus get rid of all self-made prisons. He says: The only true statement is 'I am'. All else is mere inference. By no effort can you change the 'I am' into 'I am-not'.

Behold, the real experiencer is not the mind, but myself, the light in which everything appears. Self is the common factor at the root of all experience, the awareness in which everything happens. The entire field of consciousness is only as a film, or a speck, in 'I am'. This 'I am-ness' is, being conscious of consciousness, being aware of itself. And it is indescribable, because it has no attributes. It is only being my self, and being my self is all that there is. Everything that exists, exists as my self. There is nothing which is different from me. There is no duality and, therefore, no pain. There are no problems. It is the sphere of love, in which everything is perfect. What happens, happens spontaneously, without intentions – like digestion, or the growth of the hair. Realize this, and be free from the limitations of the mind.

Behold, the deep sleep in which there is no notion of being this or that. Yet 'I am' remains. And behold the eternal now. Memory seems to bring things to the present out of the past, but all that happens does happen in the present only. It is only in the timeless now that phenomena manifest themselves. Thus, time and causality do not apply in reality. I am prior to the world, body and mind. I am the sphere in which they appear and disappear. I am the source of them all, the universal power by which the world with its bewildering diversity becomes manifest.

In spite of its primevality, however, the sense of 'I am' is not the Highest. It is not the Absolute. The sense, or taste of 'I am-ness' is not absolutely beyond time. Being the essence of the five elements, it, in a way, depends upon the world. It arises from the body, which, in its turn, is built by food, consisting of the elements. It disappears when the body dies, like the spark extinguishes when the incense stick burns out. When pure awareness is attained, no need exists any more, not even for 'I am', which is but a useful pointer, a direction-indicator towards the Absolute. The awareness 'I am' then easily ceases. What prevails is that which cannot be described, that which is beyond words. It is this 'state' which is most real, a state of pure potentiality, which is prior to everything. The 'I am' and the universe are mere reflections of it. It is this reality which a *jnani* has realized.

The best that you can do is to listen attentively to the *jnani* – of whom Sri Nisargadatta is a living example – and to trust and believe him. By such listening you will realize that his reality is your reality. He helps you in seeing the nature of the world and of the 'I am'. He urges you to study the workings of the body and the mind with solemn and intense concentration, to recognize that you are neither of them and to cast them off. He suggests that you return again and again to 'I am' until it is your only abode, outside of which nothing exists; until the ego as a limitation of 'I am' has disappeared. It is then that the highest realization will just happen effortlessly.

Mark the words of the *jnani,* which cut across all concepts and dogmas. Maharaj says: "until one becomes self-realized, attains to knowledge of the self, transcends the self, until then, all these cock-and-bull stories are provided, all these concepts." Yes, they are concepts, even 'I am' is, but surely there are no concepts more precious. It is for the seeker to regard them with the utmost seriousness, because they indicate the Highest Reality. No better concepts are available to shed all concepts.

I am thankful to Sudhakar S. Dikshit, the editor, for inviting me to write the Foreword to this new edition of I AM THAT and thus giving me an opportunity to pay my homage to Sri Nisargadatta Maharaj, who has expounded the highest knowledge in the simplest, clearest and the most convincing words.

Douwe Tiemersma
Philosophical Faculty

Erasmus University
Rotterdam, Holland June, 1981

2.4 Experiencing non-duality

March 11, 2001 in Heerenveen

[Silence]

Stay alert, while you sit so wonderfully still and everything is open.

Each time you stop thinking there is that silence. Internally you can be aware of it. You sit down, the relaxation comes, the silence comes, the recognition comes.

It can be that it remains totally silent. That's beautiful.

But, as many say, after a period of time thoughts begin to circulate again and everything continues on in the old way. Experiences, memories and expectations start to function and you begin thinking. How is that possible in the silence? Apparently because you don't stay sufficiently aware in that empty silence.

So, stay so internally alert within yourself that you experience: now there is absolutely nothing and it is good. Only then is everything good.

This sphere is present in the here and now. But the here and now is always and everywhere. You walk towards this building; you see the crocus blossoming and you hear the birds; it's spring. In complete silence and emptiness it's perfect just as it is.

You can become aware of this by yourself and continually confirm it more clearly within. That ultimate that you've always sought, is always very clearly present in your own sphere. When you remain alert, you see it at once because it's completely empty. You notice that the thinking stops, that there is nothing and that a little later thinking starts back up again. In the interim period, there was no form, no thought, no image.

Then usually you reconnect to the thought forms that were present in memory before the emptiness, and thinking goes on again in the old way. Then you haven't learned from it when it was really quiet.

When you remain lucid, there arises an internal being-knowledge of the silence. As you stay internally aware, you clearly confirm that there is no thinking and that there is no one who is thinking. In the silence you are present no longer as a person, but as being-awareness. Internally, you can verify this very clearly. When you are very alert, you can see the old forms slowly returning and you don't go along with them. Emptiness is not disturbed by forms.

Many go seeking after the silent wholeness when their own situation is not looking so good. But don't let yourself be carried away by your own thoughts and feelings. Examine your situation. Then the problems continue to disappear.

The main point of this inquiry is that you remain alert, consciously present. That same consciousness then appears to be the core of the wholeness that you sought. The method of inquiry into the problematic 'I' has the solution already within it: being-awareness. It is the most important element that every person has: consciousness, consciousness of self. We say that it's typically human that we can think about ourselves, talk about ourselves. That's true, but very frequently that power is abused to create all sorts of problems: "I have this difficulty" and: "I'd just like to have a better situation". Don't look at it like a difficult thinker, but rather as being-awareness present without problems.

Thinking regularly falls away, during the day when there is an idle period and at night in your dreamless sleep. When a piece of inner clarity remains, you confirm that in this situation there is no more 'I'. There are no more 'I'-thoughts, every worry concerning that 'I' has disappeared. Again and again you see that this concern about the 'I', this 'I'-centeredness, falls away.

That 'I'-tension must surely be absent on a regular basis

otherwise you'd be dead tired. People who are totally wrapped up in it become overwrought. The 'I'-tension frequently functions continually in ordinary work. Through it you want to achieve something. Even if it's not for yourself, still you want to do something, so you set yourself to it. That's the most common structure of Western thought and action and we find it to be a natural situation.

When there is a void, it is said that there's absolutely nothing and that then no experience is possible. But the point is that you can thoroughly experience this emptiness no longer as a person – who is not there anymore – but as being-awareness. 'You without form' still confirms: yes, this is it. When you are very happy, then every structure of 'I'-being falls away. And still, internally you confirm: this is it.

When the all-embracing, the wholeness, the non-duality is present you no longer have anything to do with a person and its 'I'-tension. That has disappeared, while in an aware manner the non-duality remains. This sphere is not different from yourself. That's why this sphere is traditionally called the Self. You experience that this is indeed your own sphere, independent of all forms, free from all ideas. You are that Self in the highest degree, much more so than the forms that you have created for yourself. It is also *ānanda,* the overwhelming, intense sphere of happiness. It is so intense and so universal, that it's obvious: this is true happiness, free from all conditions, not limited by forms.

This is not something you can achieve through certain methods. In methods you have a mediation of means that should be helpful towards achieving the final goal. But this cannot be when it comes to the absolute. Every tool or path therefore is an obstacle. A path is a means towards reaching a particular destination. Then there is the structure: starting point, path and goal. Everything is defined by the place it occupies within this structure. When the goal cannot be defined because it is empty, there is no path, and also there is no method. The only thing you can do is sit down and let everything relax. Then everything falls away.

Yet still there is something that remains. What? It is that from which the forms emerge and disappear once again. And you still confirm: I am that self in the highest degree. They can take everything away from me and what remains is: This. This is always present; you don't have to search for it anywhere. It is always the foundation of everything that is, also the foundation of your own form. The forms arise within it and disappear once again. And it clearly remains, as long as the lucidity remains. Then let happen whatever will happen. It no longer matters. Conditions have nothing to do with Self-being. You are free.

2.5 Everyone knows non-dual openness

From various introductory remarks and talks

In the previous sections there were quite a few references to experiences that have to do with non-duality. Many of them are not everyday experiences. Yet lots of people have memories of intense moments in which their own space broke open. The moments are perhaps rare in their stronger form. Less demonstrative experiences are more common, although their effect can be no less far-reaching. But because they remain on the margins of consciousness, usually they are not clearly recognized. They stay there due to their transparent character as well as to the refined quality of the content of the experience. They all have to do with relaxation. With every relaxation tension disappears. Tension exists between poles with a pressure-curve between them. There is distance and separation. Even with the tension that exists in the attempt to bring the poles together, the separation remains. In relaxation the separation disappears. See how natural relaxation is. Relaxation occurs automatically when tension is released. Then non-duality becomes automatically visible. So the being-experience of it is not just for individuals who have undergone a long and exhaustive training as it is often said.

Below are a number of pointers. The following chapters seek to fully clarify them. Therefore, the descriptions here are brief. They can bring a recognition of your own experiences. This recognition can become permanent, because non-duality is the ever-present foundation of existence.

Each evening the 'I'-structure with all its separations falls away when you go to sleep. When you lay down to sleep and yet remain somewhat clear internally, you feel the forms of the world, of your mind and of yourself falling away. You sink down into a deep relaxation and the feeling that it's good. Then there can be a sense of the groundless and the absence of any separation with it. In dreamless sleep every fixed structure falls away. The notion of the groundless can also be present in the morning, when you awaken very slowly (see § 2.2). The groundless then is the origin from which the world, and you as a person, are created anew step-by-step. You feel that you've slept really well, without dreams. It was a dreamless sleep with a wonderful sphere of inseparability in which you participated. Everything appears to emerge from this openness.

When you pay attention to it, it becomes clear that the thinking process stops at different times during the day. You look at the clouds in the sky or the waves on the water and the mind stops its thought-activity. Then there are only clouds or waves without an 'I see' and 'I think'. Your self-being is absorbed into the undivided sphere. Sometimes there is only an undivided emptiness. Someone asks you, "What were you thinking about?" and you answer, "Nothing." These short or long periods of emptiness are often not noticed, precisely because they are empty. The mind can't do anything with them, because there is no content requiring attention. There is literally nothing to remember. That's why events preceding the emptiness become associated with the current experience to form a seemingly unbroken course in time. 'Nothing' falls outside of reality, until you are clearly aware of that nothing. This nothingness then remains in the experience of everyday life.

The flowing together of self and world frequently happens with children. The tension of the dualistic 'I'-world is not yet strongly crystallized into an irrefutable thought pattern. Sometimes memories resurface from early childhood (see § 2.1 and § 2.2): small details arise, of the carpet or wallpaper of the room, the sand in the sandbox, and so on. The thrust of this approach can go partway, but can also easily continue until the image of yourself merges into something that is indescribable.

In your desires you recognize that the original non-duality was always already present in you. The desire expressed itself in different ways. Many of them were supported by the people surrounding you. But you see the relativity of all forms and remain with your deep unfulfilled desire. You recognize the cause: your dependence on forms that are by definition limited, while your desire itself is unlimited. In every limited desire there is the infinite longing for unity with everything and everyone, for the disappearance of all separations.

When something occurs along these lines, there is joy and happiness. When borders disappear, happiness arises by itself. Happiness is without boundaries. Everyone knows this happiness. Everyone knows it, if only by sensing its absence. Then there is the striving to find it again. The knowledge of happiness doesn't come from outside, but from within. This knowledge of happiness and happiness itself exist within your own self-being. You are that.

This is clear in complete enjoyment. When you are in a beautiful landscape and you enjoy the colors and shapes, or when you taste something really delicious, you can merge into it, that is, the separation between yourself and what you perceive falls away. Then the non-duality is quite clear. That's also the case when two people who love each other come together in their lovemaking and through an orgasm merge into universal non-duality.

This universality of non-dual openness becomes especially clear when the very solid limits of normal life are transcended through feeling awareness: the limits of life and the human situation. Everyone has to deal with death and the hard limits of the human possibility. The notion of a frontier is always accompanied by the sense that there is something on the other side of that fence. From a notion or being-experience of the space beyond these limits an acceptance of the human world can arise such that the separations fall away. There can even be the being-experience of unity with the transcendent and of unity with the transcendent and the world.

Everyone appears to have an awareness and some experience of the non-dual openness. People frequently overlook it or forget the experience as it was. When this experience is found to be so important that the focus remains there, that the dimension remains open, there is a spontaneous development of the experiential content. Then the openness manifests itself in a complete manner.

Reflections on the Snekermeer
The emptiness of lake and meadow's green
flows out into
the emptiness in myself.

The height of the blue sky
shears open the depth
of body, water and land.

The abundance of light
floods the world
to brilliant gold and

overexposes
my form.

In this great transformation
bewilderment seizes me
and causes my
trembling.

In the groundless release
light unfolds itself endlessly;
universal happiness
tears open.

The open space of land and sea
becomes so strongly my own:
bright light and happiness
as myself.

Finally home;
always home.

3

The non-duality of situations

In the different situations of life there appear to be different viewpoints and realities. They are valued in different ways. The non-dual openness, in which all situations have a place, each viewpoint and every reality, seems to deserve the highest valuation.

3.1 The trees

Commentary on a Taoist text, requested through the e-mail magazine Amigo, July 2002

The Text

When I was a child trees were trees,
people, people, and horses were horses.
The air was the air and the sun was the sun.
Then I went searching and became spiritual.
Then trees were people, people were the sun.
The sun became clouds and the clouds, water.
Now I've found myself again,
trees are again trees and the sun is the sun
people are once again people,
a cloud again a cloud.

Commentary

"When I was a child", the trees were not just trees, but the home of the wind and the birds, and the shadow through which the sunlight played.

When I became an adult, trees became organisms made of wood and vessels with bark, trunks and green leaves, the source of oxygen for animals and men.

"Then I went searching" and the trees became myself; my leaves rustle and my branches blow in the wind. They also shrink into a distant place in the space of my being-awareness.

Now trees are all these things simultaneously: magical beings, hard matter, identical to me, a representation, idea… nothing, and so accordingly I too have these aspects. Any statement about trees and about me is, through its one-sidedness, an error; everything can be said about it.

With a child I talk about elves in the hollow of a tree trunk, with adults on the mechanism of carbon dioxide assimilation, with seekers on the tree-being itself and on the tree as a projected image. The openness is all of this simultaneously, while it remains the Openness.

This is inexpressible.

3.2 What is reality?

From various talks, Gouda, end of 2003

You ask the question, "What is reality?" because the reality you currently experience is no longer so solid. Apparently the familiar reality is not the sole and fixed reality for you. Otherwise you wouldn't be asking about the nature of reality. That's a good starting point for further investigation.

How does reality come into existence?

In life as a small child you learn quite practically what reality is. Reality is what is hard and has its own existence. The wall is hard when your head bumps against it and the ground is hard when you fall. Other people are hard if they don't agree with you or don't have kind feelings for you. Luck is hard when you have an accident. This creates the notion of an external, hard reality that is separate from yourself.

The many realities

You have experienced that reality is not only hard, but that its character can also change. You know different realms, such as the great space of consciousness, the everyday working environment and the dream world. It's good to consciously see the various sorts of reality. As a child you live in a different world than you do as an adult. Sometimes you experience a more emotional sphere, sometimes a more rationally ordered world. With illness there is another reality than with health. When you look at other people inside and outside of your own cultural sphere you notice that the variety of realities is quite great.

Some time ago there was an interview on TV with an old farmer who claimed that the earth was flat. The journalist found it amusing to make him look ridiculous. But the farmer had just as much right as the journalist who claimed that the earth was round. Both of them had empirical arguments. On the vast beach of Schiermonnikoog the earth is as flat as a pancake; if you travel in space, it's a round ball. In either case you take into account the specific reality that you experience. Each situation is real according to its corresponding viewpoint. But just take the multitude of realities seriously. Then that breaks through the simplistic adherence to one well-known reality. So an openness arises.

Initially it can seem to be very chaotic when the experienced reality breaks open. Anything is possible. For example the ground on which you stand is no longer so firm, the far distance becomes near, or your body becomes a refined substance. Some people become dizzy, but that's a very positive sign. It indicates that you are no longer stuck in your old ordered reality. You become dizzier and more nauseous the harder you hold onto the old order. You will need to release your connection with the reality that you know. When you accept the chaos, it's not a problem. The chaotic waves may still continue for a while, but then they slowly calm down; in any case the dizziness disappears. Then there arises a sense of the original space within which the different worlds rise and fall. That is what precedes every experienced reality, the silent openness. Keep everything open. Then openness manifests itself.

The dependence of the reality upon the perceiver

Your position as perceiver is therefore decisive to the reality that you experience. The nature of every reality corresponds to a certain kind of perceiver. When the perceiver changes, the reality changes. The condition of the perceiver can change in all different kinds of components and aspects. For example, the eyes may function less well, but instruments such as glasses or a microscope can then expand the field of vision. There is a huge variation in the senses and in their associated worlds of the animal kingdom. What is the reality of a boar that can hardly see anything, but smells everything with his snout? What is the world of a bat who perceives his prey with a type of echo-apparatus in the dark? The situation of a human being is only one of the many possibilities. Bees experience the rose that we see in a very different way. If you had the eyes of a bee, your world would look very different. You would not know about the world that we humans experience. As a child I was always very amazed at this. You see the construction of reality already on the biological level. This biological conditioning is so strong that people experience their world as fixed. Of course, if you always look through your eyes, you always see roses in approximately the same way. Nevertheless this rose-reality depends upon our biological foundation. The psychological factors of feeling, mood, orientation, and current knowledge all allow the construction to be seen more clearly. Depending upon what you've learned in life and depending on your attitudes, you experience a certain reality. In experience and thus in the experienced reality there is a great conditioning. Reality is dependent upon the perceiver.

However, the world was not created by the human mind. It's

nonsense to say that "the world is in the mind" or "I create reality". The mind is not all powerful. Like the body and its world, the mind is a temporary and conditioned phenomenon. In every situation there are two poles: the one who knows and that which is known, subject and object. The two always go together. Whenever the one changes, the other changes too. There is interdependence, relativity. There is a mutual engagement of subject and object, of knowledge and being. They arise together, interact and disappear once again.

See through the conditioning and its relativity. Then you experience the conditioned realities with their limitations. Then the obsession and attachment to them disappears. Then there develops an always larger open sphere, in which less and less conditions arise. Everything is possible; all options remain open. There is even an openness for the absence of any reality. That is the situation prior to every creation. That is the Origin without form and without qualities, from which all creations as new realities arise and disappear once again.

Higher and lower realities

Do you see the many realities and their relativity? Still, different situations receive a different valuation in terms of the character of their reality. You find one more real than the other. From a new perspective you can sometimes clearly confirm the limits of an old reality. When you awaken, you can immediately see that the dream was actually a lower form of reality than the awakened one. You say: "Oh, it was only a dream. Now I am awake." Another well-known example is that of the snake and the rope. If you are in the tropics and almost step on a snake in the semi-darkness, you shout out loud, especially if it appears to be a very poisonous one. Afterwards when the light is turned on and you see that it's only a rope lying there, the snake reality immediately receives a lower valuation relative to the rope reality. The latter is the higher reality. In the succession of realities it is frequently confirmed what a higher reality is and what a lower reality is. This confirmation is a direct recognition with the criteria of 'more light' or 'more awareness'. It is a direct insight: "Yes, there is more light and now I know it; the other was but a dream, imagination, illusion." There is no doubt any longer. What was reality at first becomes relative in the light of another reality. This other reality is directly experienced as a 'higher' reality. Usually there is a clear difference between degrees of more or less appearance and between degrees of reality. Therefore the criteria are how much light there is, or the spaciousness of the view, such as when you climb a mountain.

It seems to me very difficult to confirm that something is real. It could also be the pinnacle of illusion.

You can do nothing other than continuing to watch as attentively as possible, with the widest view that you can manage, as critical as possible, and also with respect to yourself. Then you see that illusions are caused by a limited viewpoint. When you confirm that you have a more expansive view of everything than you previously did, you make a distinction between a lower and a higher reality. Through being self-critical you can return to your most lucid form of consciousness and see through many limitations and illusions.

And don't stop too soon. People often find a great perspective when they come across a good spiritual idea, for example with the notion that the soul does not die but reincarnates. You see the limitations of that position and that reality when you let everything dissolve in a greater space.

I just said that there is a mutual link between perceiver and reality. In a practical sense there is still a primacy of the perceiver, not as a perceiver with a perception device, but rather its capacity as being-awareness. In every situation, in every reality, you have the possibility to rise above that situation in consciousness. This impetus can proceed. Your point of view can free itself again and again from a reality that has become relative due to a new point of view from a higher perspective. For example, after the transition from dream to waking, the waking state can also be seen as a dream compared to an even more awake state. This can be directly recognized.

The 'highest'

Through a backwards movement in your consciousness you can always absorb a higher point of view. This means that you release everything that appears in experience, that you release yourself, so that the old identities with their conditionings no longer play a role. How far can this go? As long as there is still conditioning, however subtle, there is a limitation in the perspective and in the experienced world. When every condition, every form of self and world is released, there is no restrictive framework any longer. Then there is the recognition of the original unconditioned 'state'. What kind of 'perspective' is that? This 'perspective' makes everything relative, although it can no longer be made relative through an even higher position. There is no position any longer, because there are no forms and no properties. There is nothing more to be overcome which could then become susceptible to relativization. 'That' has no form and cannot be grasped. It cannot be formulated, because defining involves both demarcation and transcendence.

That 'viewpoint' is yourself. It is the non-objectifiable depth of each person, of each living being, of all that is. You have knowledge of it. You were always present as the highest self while other realities manifested, during all transformations of your reality, when the ground became waves, when the chasm appeared, when you understood the relativity of all types of reality. You were always yourself, unchangeable, the groundless source of all phenomena. You were that and you remain that as consciousness without form and without borders. That is your identity as openness. Without you as being-awareness things could not appear. You are that light which all things need in order to appear. Creation arises within it. You have no need of any other light to exist because you are the groundless Light.

Creation and illusion

When there is a specific world selling itself as absolute reality, you can immediately confirm it as an invitation to self-delusion. It is a conjured reality which is not real. It's a magic trick that you step into when you don't see through the trick clearly enough. The art of the conjurer lies not so much in the learning of a certain sleight of hand and manipulation of things, but rather in the skill of placing people in such a position so as to see another reality and not the trick. Therefore the magician always tells nice stories. People see a wonderful reality. Of course they know that it's an illusory reality. That knowledge means retaining a more solid reality in which it's impossible to be sawn in half and afterwards spring up again, alive on the stage. From a higher perspective you see the trick. You have the same thing with what the school-master and others have conjured for you and you have accepted as reality. You have accepted so many things as a matter of course. From your higher being-awareness you clearly see that what you learned is relative and that your belief in it as absolute was an illusion. Every absolute faith in a situation is an illusion. When you take something with name and form as absolute, you confuse the absolute and relative with one another. This is an illusion, a mistaken belief in some form which you take to be a reality. You see the illusion when the forms become transparent. A child with a monster mask approaches you and wants to frighten you. But the mask is transparent and you smile. Later, if someone with authority says something to you, you sit trembling and believe everything he says.

Of course, everything can continue naturally. Only accept the reality which appears before your eyes. The phenomena that are there are there. They are there as phenomena, no more and no less. They can be there, but they don't have restrictive power on you any longer. You see how the magician conjures and you can smile at it. You see a child conjuring very seriously; you smile and play along with the game. From the feeling of openness, there is an infinite love and there is compassion for the suffering that people inadvertently cause themselves, because they experience the limited as unlimited. For adults life isn't a game because it's about a 'solid reality'. You see others talking very seriously, but you experience the infinite space and you smile.

Don't you disqualify science in this way?

I disqualify science only to the extent that it pretends to go beyond the limits of its scope. When you assert something you should always be aware of the limits of that assertion, and that is determined by the type of the subject-object relationship. The borders appear to be very narrow. There are also the truths of visual art, of literature, of religion, and so on. We have talked about the body. What is the truth of the body?

I don't know.

Me neither. You can say anything about it. You can say something about cells, tissues, organs, but that requires a certain attention. Before you know it, you're speaking with others dead seriously, as if these constructions are the only reality. Return to where you came from – then you know what reality is.

3.3 Viewpoints

Gouda, December 7, 2005

You are sitting down and it's become quiet. Relaxation comes and your entire field of consciousness clears. With relaxation the clarity increases by itself.

You become more aware of yourself in the whole situation. This happens naturally when you take some distance from your physical circumstances. It can also occur when you happily sit and relax. The limitations, the fogs, they disappear so easily.

There exists a more spacious sphere in which you are very aware of yourself, also of your own situation.

Take a look once again at your own circumstances. You are here; but in what way? In which way are you here? Is there a further interpretation of 'I-am'? If so, take a look at the nature of that interpretation. Usually there is a center of perception and action. That center is an 'I'-center: "I do this", "I do that", "I see this", "I feel that". Along with it comes identification with, among other things, your body. Actually, it is an identification with an image of your body, an idea of what your body is. There's also an identification with a self-image, a picture of yourself as a person. How is it now with that 'I', 'my-self', identified with all these images?

When you look precisely, that 'I' appears to be nothing more than a point of view. Tonight it's good to look once again at your viewing point. Every position has a perspective. Every position has a certain world. Take a look once again at the most common situation where you take your identity to be the body. Usually you look out towards the world from a place somewhere behind your eyes. That is a particular location that immediately creates an orientation of before-behind, left-right, top-bottom. When things come towards you, they come towards that position where you are present. When you take a position in your head, then all sorts of things become fixed, such as what is front and back, what is near and far, what approaches and what recedes. So if the identification with that viewing point in your head is very strong, then your fortunes in relation to that structure are immediately clear. You are in the world of hearing, seeing and other experiences. You are fully engaged in that world.

See that viewing point as explained by the laws of perspective. You see both sides of the long, straight road merging in the distance and vice versa as all sightlines return back to you. One vanishing point is in the distance, the other vanishing point is there in your head, where you are. When you are small, you have a low perspective; when you grow up you have a higher perspective with a wider horizon. We have frequently spoken about this before: go out and stand at the top of a cathedral. Suddenly there is a very different point of view, a very different perspective, a very different world. Notice that whatever position you take, it's not neutral. As a small child you have a low position, so you have a low perspective. What appears there is usually so unbelievably large that you always feel quite small. When you stand at the top of a tower you see the little cars moving and the tiny people walking below. That's a completely different perspective. But that also means another identity. Take a look for example at: "I am small and they are big", "they will always hurt me", or alternatively: "you've got to see this, the grand view, the wide horizon and the mass of humanity down there, the people look like ants". Look once again into your own sphere and see what it's like with respect to the different viewpoints and the corresponding different identities. You can absorb all the different points of view. What you see depends on your own viewing point; but also, what your own identity is. What do you see? Now, just tell me... Then I know what your identity is there. The complement to your story, you are that. That is your viewpoint; that is yourself, as viewpoint.

You can't just say: I create everything. That's nonsense. You can only say that the two poles, self-being and world, are directly linked. Each viewpoint has its own world, its own perspective. So what you experience as reality is dependent upon your own viewpoint. In this sense the world is relative, related to and so dependent upon your own viewpoint. Every pronouncement that you make about a situation immediately has as its complement a viewpoint. Every judgment again has as complement that viewpoint in yourself. Every statement says at least as much about yourself as about the world.

You have all kinds of viewpoints. You have viewpoints with a very restricted view, a very limited horizon. You have higher viewpoints and then the horizon is wider. What is the highest viewpoint?

No viewpoint.

If you can realize what that really means... But, let's look again at the viewpoints, because insight into them is so important. What is the highest viewpoint?

But first let me pose an interim question: what is a really high viewpoint? (laughter)

The cathedral with its overview.

We've already been up there.

[Another] A viewpoint which accepts all other viewpoints.

Now, that's not a bad idea. You can even sit on the moon, for example. Then you see the Earth arise with its atmosphere and its continents. And billions of people walking there, each with their own viewpoint. And those viewpoints are not the same, so then they fight with one another. But you see how relative all viewpoints really are. It's crazy to massacre one another because of a relative viewpoint. So by taking a greater distance you can see the different limited positions. You see them in their relativity.

But the moon isn't really so far away. We can take it to the end. Suppose we have an interstellar mission, millions of light years away. Fortunately, time is also relative, so it's possible. And then we look around. What is the earth? Less than a particle of dust. Good, let's go a bit further: you are sitting on the roof of the universe. You can't go any further, because beyond the boundaries of the universe space ceases to exist. So viewpoints aren't there any more. We are sitting on the roof, on the edge of the universe. You can say that we certainly have the last viewpoint there. But: just remain sitting there. You can do nothing more. What happens then?

Dissolving.

Yes. When you really stay there, you also feel the constriction of that last viewpoint dissolve. Experience that very concretely. It is the last viewing point, the viewpoint of the witness. There are hardly any personal elements left. There is just a viewpoint of seeing, of sight itself. In that border region you are aware of yourself as witness, of yourself as the last viewpoint in space. In that viewpoint there is still a clear perspective: you are the witness of phenomena. The phenomena are seen within that perspective. When you do vipassana meditation, you are the witness of phenomena and there is still a clear perspective. When you become aware of yourself as witnessing consciousness in space, and when you stay there on that edge, you'll also find that that last viewpoint also dissolves... into the inexpressible.

That inexpressible can remain consciously present together with all those viewpoints and worlds. That inexpressible can remain as both the context and the center in which everything appears and disappears. That is the non-dual openness. [...]

But surely there are particular viewpoints and perspectives needed in order to survive.

Self-being and the urge to survive are mostly entwined together. When you are free, you are free of survival.

What is survival? You speak of survival like an organism trying to stay alive under difficult circumstances and with the help of various strategies. When you are truly free, it really has nothing to do with an individual life that must further itself. Without a viewpoint life appears to be free and takes care of itself, as long as it's there. Life lives itself, including all the biological mechanisms.

Then does the viewpoint-less know the reproductive drive?

No, not in the sense of an 'I' that experiences the sex drive instinct with everything that goes along with it. For as long as there is life, life lives itself. That happens with its own order of laws, but also with an awareness of all aspects of life and coexistence. So life lives itself in an egocentric-free way, while being open to all biological, psychological and social forces that are operating. You are that life and you are free of it. You can say up front that it goes so much better than with an 'I' that always has blinders on.

Does life live itself from within this order of laws, or independent of it?

These are the natural laws of life. So they are present in life. But that's not a problem. You yourself are universal life and you are free.

You see that life, precisely when it isn't artificially constrained and distorted by an 'I', develops unexpectedly.

You can't avoid those laws?

Understand what you are. For as long as there is life, there are the laws of life, apparently. You don't dictate them in advance. They are there apparently. For example, that organisms arise somewhere, grow, flourish, decay and disappear once again. So, that belongs to life. But that's not a problem. The problem comes when an 'I' wants to interfere with it, identify with this piece of life and not with that. Then everything that happens with this piece of life happens exclusively with yourself. That's the source of suffering.

But can't we avoid identification?

Just start with your situation as it is. Then you are aware of all the different possibilities and of your freedom. There is a recognition that you aren't glued to a limited identification, to one viewpoint with a large limitation. You coincide with the whole rich reality, with all viewpoints.

I still have an emotional bond with my parents. Is that then identification?

It depends on what that connection is like. You see that the relationship between parents and children can be very stifling. That 'bond' can also be experienced in the great unity of self-being. Then you are your parents, too. This means that the old level of the connection between you as an 'I'-person and your parents becomes strongly relative. Opening the connection up means releasing them, but also loving them so much that you become them. On the level of life everything is inclusive, so too, the feeling of love for your parents. Because there is no limitation in that open space, there is no problem with all the things of living and dying, with everything that arises in life.

3.4 Situations in a V-model

Library Theater, Rotterdam, December 9, 2004

The model

It can be useful to look at what I call the V-model. Within it are represented the possible distances between yourself as subject of perception and action (first person) and the object (third person) towards which you are focused. There may be a clear distance between the two, such as in observing from a distance (1), but this can also decrease (2) such as in a loving relationship, and even disappear (3).

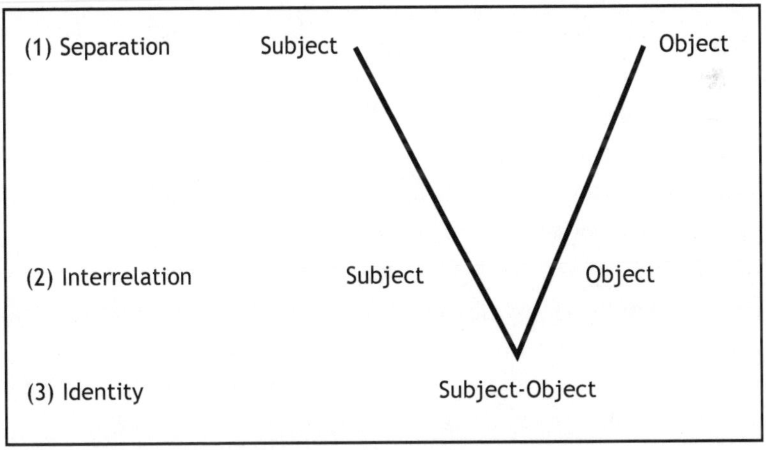

Figure 3.4-1 The V-model of existence

It can be instructive to work from the model top to bottom simply as an exercise.

As a starting point take observing from a distance (1). You

look from a distance, for example at a wall. Then let your attention return towards yourself in your body and let yourself relax. Sink further and further down and let yourself relax even more. Through this you become more open and allow things to come towards you; the distance disappears (2) and things are present within the realm of your own feeling consciousness. Ultimately there is a merging (3). This happens every night when you go to sleep. The reverse occurs when you awake in the morning, but also in the first years of life. The model then is a dynamic model: the center of gravity of self-being can lie at any level of the model and can also move.

Nevertheless, these possibilities can be recognized as permanent fundamental structures of your existence. In daily life there is an interconnectedness of everything, but usually this is not fully conscious. The fundamental unity falls almost entirely outside of your consciousness. However, all these processes can be recognized in your own actual experience.

Psychological disorder and spiritual development

So we can re-examine the stages of the emergence of a psychological disorder and of spiritual development.

a) The events that have the greatest impact on your life take place in an environment where there is a strong involvement of yourself with other people. There is not a strong objectification, nor strong separation between self and non-self, but rather a certain degree of symbiosis (2). Then there is an openness towards the other, an interconnection, a shared identity within the individual experience. When something happens there, for example the loss of someone who was important to you, a strong objectification or an attack of someone, the individual self-sphere becomes shocked. That shock can be so strong that the emotional energies become restricted and even remain in a cramped, restricted state. When these pieces or blocks of energy remain in the core of your self-being then you become stuck and this causes a long-term restriction in your life. In this way the experiences on the level of interrelation, especially those from childhood, can easily continue to play a role in adult life.

b) The limitations and cramps of self on level (1) we call 'ego'. The ego wants to maintain itself against the forces that attack its own sense of order. The so-called complexes on level (2) create instability, so they are suppressed as much as possible. Frequently this doesn't work. As soon as the familiarly ordered world disappears, there is fear: "I don't want to be ruined"; "I don't want to die". There is a tendency to return to the known order of level (1), to maintain the 'I' so that the fear will disappear. When that doesn't work there is a further cramping of the 'I' on level (2). This is very clear in a strongly depressed personality disorder. On level (1) it can also result in an even further withdrawal, which is clear in the schizoid disorder. It can always continue further. Then the 'I' stands at an even greater distance in an ever-increasing space. Because that space is more and more terrifying, the cramping also increases. The person is stuck turning in upon himself in an ever shrinking circle, with the danger that everything will implode into a psychosis. How to come out of that?

c) One solution to the problem can sometimes come from a shift back to (1). In the course of a lifetime much of your childhood can be objectified. Then you take distance from your previous experiences of self and world and you are free of it. The deeper the experiences go, the harder it is to release them. In heavily loaded emotional experiences, it often seems totally impossible. Then there is the way 'downwards', to literally descend as an aware self-being to a level that lies deeper, that is, previous to the level on which the emotional complex was created. As the self-being discovers itself there in the pre-traumatic depth of awareness, the issue truly disappears. In the spacious sphere of the original being-awareness the stuck energies can unravel themselves in space, develop and resolve.

It's about a regression from the level of cognitive organization (1) towards the sphere in which self and non-self interpenetrate one another. Also later for adults this return is possible because the open unity (3) as foundation is always already present. This means that the cramping, the grasping onto energetic structures, falls away, so that there is a surrender of the ego, a release of the 'I' into the All-Encompassing. Trust is necessary for that. Therefore, a being-experience of encompassing love is decisive. Thus, there can be an awareness of the possibilities of (1), (2) and (3), an awareness and an acceptance that there are three levels of separation and unity simultaneously present. That is inseparability, non-duality, advaita.

Therefore what happens when fear arises from the breaking through of the limits of the normal world is crucial. Either there is a grasping onto the ego and a further reaction in the form of a cramp, or there is surrender. In the latter case there is a spiritual breakthrough and existential psychological healing.

The negative way

The flowing together in the movement towards the point at the bottom of the V-model (3) is a unification in being. In the advaita tradition there is also another movement towards unity, namely through taking distance, a distance which is as great as possible between subject and object. In the line of the left side then you move further upwards. Your viewpoint shifts up and a little to the rear; you do it as though you are stepping back. A witnessing observer arises there, a more reflexive consciousness. Through it you continually release more and more forms of yourself; you see them as objective phenomena. You remain yourself as pure awareness. The legs of the V expand upwards. The awareness-space increases.

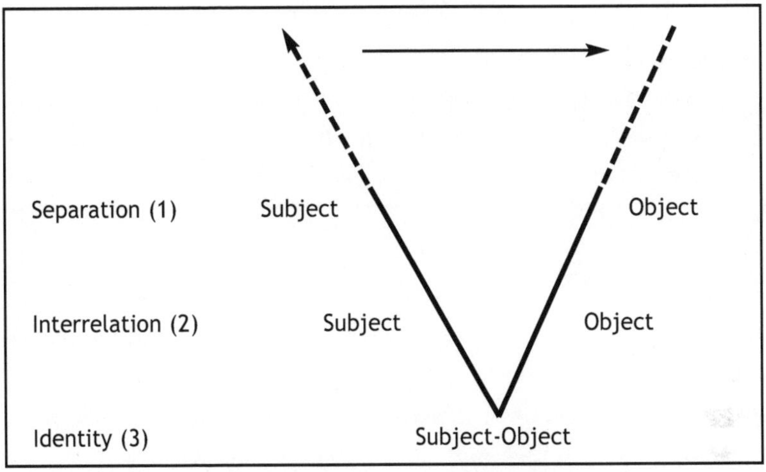

Figure 3.4-2 The 'negative' path

The Diamond model

But, what happens then? Something strange happens: the more distance you take from yourself and the things of the world, the purer your consciousness becomes, and the closer the things come to you. The consciousness space has greatly expanded. The

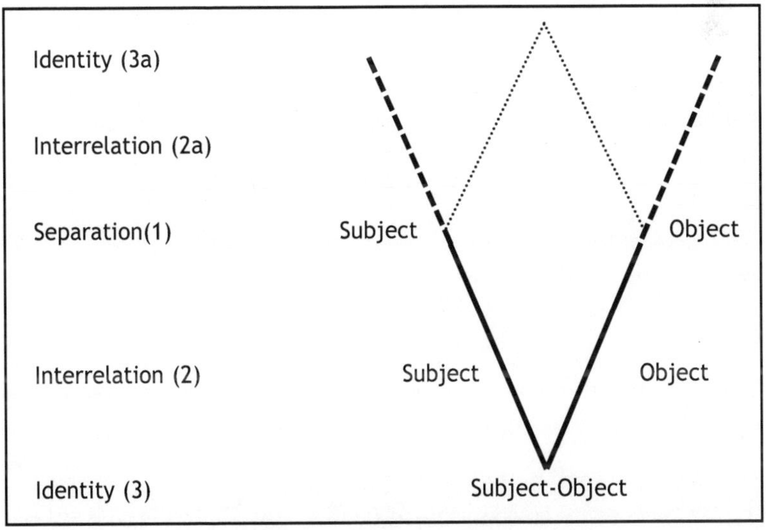

Figure 3.4-3 The diamond model

things appear more and more within it, thus within your own consciousness. Increasingly, they seem to be less different than yourself. In the V-model, this means a swinging back together of the extended legs. This process can continue until it becomes one identity of self and other. The V-model has become a diamond model.

The Wave model

Actually, with the continuing objectification of self and the purification of consciousness, the objective (the other) meets you around back. That is the Great. Unexpectedly it engulfs you, dissolving you so that you come together and merge with it. This then is the model of a wave that rises from the ocean.

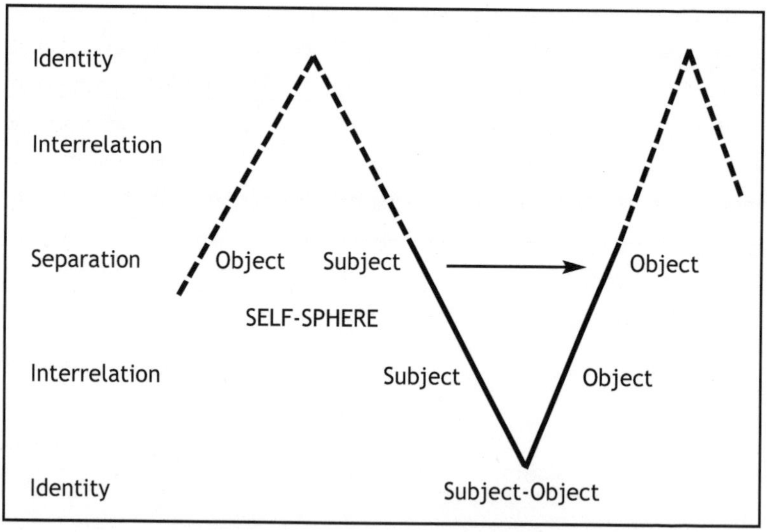

Figure 3.4-4 The wave model

You can even position yourself on the surface, focusing out towards all the external things (not-self) at a distance. There, you can also be aware that you are the whole wave, with a back side that is seen as an object by others. You can be aware of yourself as the consciousness-space above the wave. Both spheres appear to have an infinite depth: the ocean (below) and the heavens (above). Within it you have an internal connection with everything and everyone and there is simply unity. Then you let go of the limitations of your wave of existence with its small consciousness. Then there is the non-duality of non-being and being (advaita).

So non-duality is recognized everywhere subject and object come together. Initially we have seen that in relaxation by allowing yourself to sink into the depths of being (3 in the model) and secondly in the further expansion of awareness (3a). There is the third possibility that, beginning from the separated situation (1) directly on the horizontal level, the distance between yourself as an observer and the observed object can become smaller and disappear altogether. This distance-disappearance can also occur through an approach or surprise attack of the Other. When you let go of your resistance and become one with the other the great other washes over you in front, side, or back (see the Great in the wave model). This distance-disappearance can also occur by going towards the other, and accepting them as yourself. That is the unity that love brings. Both types of movement can also occur simultaneously.

With all these movements the distance between the other and yourself disappears, between the object of perception or action and yourself. Then there is a point where the two coincide. That point is a 'big bang', a huge, infinite eruption of the still, empty, clear space in which self and everything is included and within which the entire cosmos can arise once again. Even though the core structure of subject and object has disappeared, there is still a clear internal knowledge. As long as that remains, a new creation doesn't close off the open non-dual sphere. The waves that arise don't create separations within the ocean. There is no return anymore to a narrowed consciousness, no return to a limited viewpoint. Every perspective and every reality is simply allowed to be.

It is important to see that the model has only a relative value. It shouldn't be given an independent life of its own. Connecting to your own experience should and must remain. The model can be seen as a map which in a simplified form indicates the locations and ways of experiencing self-being or it can be viewed as a blueprint of the possibilities of self-being. The model offers a perspective on aspects that might otherwise be easily neglected.

3.5 The highest reality as the non-duality of situations

From various introductions and talks

Everyone seeks 'the highest'

The most important criterion to use for qualifying one point of view or truth as higher than another is the space and clarity of consciousness it brings to the individual existence. With greater space and clarity more content can increasingly reveal itself and your existence can continue to expand. The development in this direction of expansion and enlightenment means more relaxation, softness, lightness, beauty, goodness, joy, happiness. It opens up new dimensions. These qualities appear to manifest fully with the complete opening, up to the inexpressible. The worlds that belong to the various viewpoints break open and finally receive a place in the groundless openness.

Everyone values an expansion of their existence and consciousness. They seek this in a variety of ways: traveling, reading and studying, through acquiring more power or possessions, through more relationships, more experiences, etc. In science people try to develop more and more encompassing theories, that is to say, theories which can explain more phenomena than the current theories do. When it's successful in the scientific perspective there's more unity in the experienced reality. Within that one perspective the scientist sees an ever-expanding terrain from a greater height. The unity of perspective is sought as the highest value. Seeing more in your own perspective means more being.

People have become less arrogant in their attitude towards animals than previously. They see that the lives of animals are no less perfect than those of humans. Still there remains a definite appreciation for the symbolization capacity of human beings. Through this capacity humans live in a much wider world than animals do, freer and with more opportunities. In addition to the difference in biological realities, there are also the worlds of language, music, visual art, religion, etc. When considering the development of life and culture, the spaciousness of the perspective receives the highest value.

The movement towards greater space is also valued because opposites are absorbed into a larger whole and so become less important. This applies to internal psychological conflicts experienced within the wider sphere of consciousness as well as to the socio-political conflicts experienced within a wider context. For example, the various impulses from head and heart become harmonized at the level of insight in the higher (*buddhi*) mind. The conflicts between the various European states disappear with their progressive integration into the European Union. The dialectical movement towards greater unity leads to a greater whole where everything is included. This can become totalitarian. Therefore, it's not about one great unity, which always implies duality, but rather the breaking through of the groundless and inexpressible openness.

The realization of this reality means a total expansion and breaking open of the personal sphere, a release of egocentricity, group-centricity, anthropocentrism and a loving acceptance of others. Only through love do the limitations of the ego disappear allowing the infinite non-duality to reveal itself. This love is seen as very important everywhere, even though people don't come to it in order to let it define their life. Nevertheless, what we are speaking about belongs to the highest.

The highest is also expressed in people's desires. Usually desire is focused upon something limited. In desiring, you sit here and the object of your desire is over there. When you reach the desired object, the desire continues because the object of your desire is limited. It is an endless process. It shows that desire itself is infinite. Yet if you realize that and go along with your infinite desire, then what is left of you and your world? Apparently that is what you really desire, your highest desire.

When people hold on tightly to a limited situation, it's because they think that the greatest space can be found within it. Ascetics limit their desires and physical needs with the idea of winning everything. Many limit themselves because they fear that the larger space would crush them. That's the reason why many people remain in an old, limited situation. There are prisoners who have done their time in jail, yet prefer to remain in prison; there are freed slaves, who prefer to keep their old situation and agoraphobics who remain sitting in their own small rooms. Others who see from a larger perspective are unanimous about the contraction and blindness of such people. They see the restrictions and wouldn't trade their freedom for that limited situation.

Also the actions which promote segregation and which harm others must be seen as such. They arise from the notion that such actions promote unity, space and happiness. These beautiful things are reserved for one person or one group and this seems quite understandable. Then egocentricity or group-centricity is strongly present. This means that people ascribe the highest value to themselves or to what is their own. Promoting unity means that the self expands, receiving more power. Dictators say that they have the best interests of their country (that is themselves) in mind. Everyone seeks the best, at least that which is seen as the best. Everyone wants to be happy, at least that which is seen to make us happy. This image of happiness can be very limited and can function restrictively on others. The good that was sought, therefore, becomes harmful to other people. Those with a wider perspective see this very clearly.

Nevertheless, everyone seeks space, freedom and unity. These qualities remain as the highest value, even though it isn't understood that these qualities can't fully manifest until people have released themselves.

The claim of truth

The diversity of situations (viewpoints – realities) come together in 'the highest'. In experience it can be approached through a backwards motion of a progressively deeper and deeper critique, an objectification and release of the constraints with which people are imprisoned, continuing until no substantive form remains. This sphere can be known internally as the sphere of open-being and is experienced as the most undeniable thing that there is. That's not to say that a new viewpoint can't be absorbed or that a great new story can't be told which is once again relativized. There is a claim of truth, but this truth has no substantive form. The unity is not a closed system, it's not a totality; it has nothing to do with a viewpoint. What truth is cannot be formulated. It is inexpressible. Nevertheless this inexpressibly open truth can be recognized; it is recognized as being not different from yourself. It's a direct internal confirmation without a person, tools or content. Therefore there is no talk of a choice between different philosophical options in relation to the highest truth. In such a supra-personal sphere the choice-situation and the options don't exist. [...]

You ask me what the highest reality is. I wonder what sort of answer you expect. You'd like to get a clear description, but you know that every response will be insufficient. With a concrete answer you can always think of 'something higher', until you encounter the limits of language. The 'highest' lies beyond these limits. Language has no hold there. With language you can certainly indicate something, but then you can also immediately posit the opposite. Without that opposite you would have only a partial reality. When the linguistic separations that are used to distinguish between the one and the other are surrendered, the content of language is rendered meaningless. Then what remains is a reference to your feeling being-awareness beyond language.

Nevertheless there is within you a knowing, an original knowledge of the 'highest', the pure, the purely good, the beautiful, true, being, consciousness. Everyone has a certain notion of the good, etc... and this notion goes beyond the empirical experiences that people have had. There is a knowledge that happiness can be total. If you have ever experienced it yourself, you know that happiness is not a perception. It is an absorption into happiness, so that there is nothing left. There's not even experience anymore; there's only happiness. Still you have knowledge of it. That knowing continues to exist, even though your daily life may be a mess.

You are changed by getting to know this notion better and better. It is the task of the teacher to develop the vague knowing of the pupil into clear knowledge. That is the Socratic Method. Plato's ideas then should be interpreted as fields or spheres, where the subject can end up if he focuses himself upon them. There is a direct internal relationship between the first person and the idea which he increasingly recognizes as his own quality or sphere. You literally enter into the sphere of the good, the beautiful and the true. So this is an existential interpretation of his ideas. The motion of the first person goes beyond the contemplation of the heavenly spheres with pure ideas until there is no person any longer. Then there is only the universal Good, the Beautiful, the True, the Joy in which everything and everyone is absorbed. All situations are included within it, because each situation is permeated by the Good, etc... You have internal knowledge of this. Finally the inexpressible openness manifests itself there. It reveals itself abundantly clearly as the non-duality of all situations. [...]

You have a difficulty with your orientation. You are uncertain about what comes next. You have a rough idea of what you have and don't know what you will get. You have what you have, but already you say that what you have is limited. That can just fall away. What do you really have now, of which no uncertainty or doubt exists? What is the most sure? Go there to take a look.

Everyone has his own things that he is sure of.

What is the most certain? All things can fall away, even your thinking. But what can never disappear? That which you still are as your deepest self? You can clearly see that you are yourself and that nobody can take this away from you. They can, if it comes to the worst, take your body away from you, but your self-being remains. This self-being goes beyond the thinking-being that Descartes saw as the most certain. It is ultimately without form and beyond time. It has always been and will always be. Focus there and feel: "I am my Self". Everyone has that Self, everyone is that Self. It is the most certain. It is possible to doubt anything, but no one doubts their own existence. Even as all images of yourself disappear, your Self remains present. In this self-knowledge without form there is a direct confirmation that this is the indubitable truth, even if it is very subtle and refined.

There is a direct knowledge of that infinite reality, but it can't be put into words. For as long as words with substantive references are spoken, they concern relative situations and can only have a practical value and a relative truth. They only have value if they actually bring others closer to the living experience of the highest truth in which there exists a non-duality of the situations. Through that, the relativity of the words becomes automatically clear.

In the following chapters the theme of 'the highest' is developed further: first as it is experienced externally and then internally, then as the non-duality of both and finally the being-experience of the highest in various limited situations.

4

Groundless external openness

Radical non-duality means the absence of the borders and duality inherent in the person and his world. Therefore it cannot be known and brought into existence by an 'I'-person. Only from the outside can the boundaries be broken through, dissolving the quality of the 'I-am'. Through the functioning of the great external Openness, the groundless foundation of all, the depth arises in which the recognition of the identity of That and the unfathomable self can occur.

Space meditation

Take note of your attention that goes out towards external things. Then let the attention continue further in the same line through the surface of things to the horizon that you can see or imagine in the distance. Let this opening of your attention go even further by directing your gaze slightly above the horizon. Then the impulse of the attention continues on into infinity. Be clearly aware of that infinity. Experience also that this unfathomably great space turns back to you. That space encompasses everything and everyone, including yourself, even while you experience that you in your consciousness are quite large. That groundless space is present in everything and everyone, also in yourself. What does that mean?

4.1 Silence

Schiermonnikoog, February 1, 2003

You all know what the theme is this week: silence. It is here the same as it has always been: silent. Nothing has changed. Between the last time and now lies a busy life. Now, that falls away in the silence. Just let it fall. Then you notice that the silence never disappeared. When you are alert, it's very clear.

What happens in the silence? We arrive on a wintry night, with storm and snow, to a distant island and it's deathly still. What happens there with the people in the night, in the snow, at the end of the world? In the silence of the night, in the snow, in the real silence, everything dissolves, the entire group dissolves.

Take a look very precisely at how it is with yourself, where everything dissolves in the silence. Listen to the silence, listen. When the listening finds something to listen to, then there is a clear relationship between yourself on the one hand and that to which you listen on the other. Now there is the snow that keeps falling in the dark night, the snow that silently and steadily falls, and you listen. But, there is nothing that answers to the listening. There is the intention of the listening and that continues, but the silence of the snow, everywhere in the darkness, is infinite. The intention of the listening becomes infinite. You put everything into that listening for the infinite, so that nothing remains. Take a look to see exactly how it is. Listening has no grip. The energy of listening evaporates in the snow. What are you? Through listening to the sound of the snow, you are listening. As listening, you dissolve into the silence, you become the snow. There is no sound of your Self. The infinite silence remains. See how the silence dissolves everything.

They are still searching for the people of that group on the island, but haven't found them yet.

See how the silence goes beyond the contrasts of sound and silence. Usually, sound and ordinary silence alternate. You confirm that now there is sound and then again silence, then again sound. But Silence precedes this exchange. It is the original silence from which the ordinary silence and noise arise. There is a period of sound and a period of absence of sound. Sound emerges as a phenomenon, and silence emerges as a phenomenon. The source silence is always there, continuous, independent of sound and absence of sound. Go into the silence of the night, the silence of the falling snow. It's important this first evening that the original dimension of the Silence reopens.

Take note, this dimension of Silence is open now. Thus silence precedes the sounds and the silence. It precedes, just as your self precedes all phenomena. When Silence appears, you experience that it is never different from your own self-being. Silence is not a phenomenon (third person), because you are Silence (first person). When you are listening from your own self-being to the silence, you are 'listening'. Then listening coincides with the original silence; you coincide with the original silence. In that original sphere, you as silent listening, are not different from the Silence. That is meditation. Silence that listens to silence: you are That.

We put on a CD of silence, there is nothing there. We listen. 'Next track'.

If you want to listen to something, you are focused on sound. When the sound doesn't come, what happens then? Either you go back to your thoughts, or you go along into the silence. You are focused on something in your listening, and when you find nothing, the focus keeps going. So, the focus goes on and on and doesn't find any object to grasp onto. It proceeds infinitely onwards.

[Quiet music]

The music is a reference to the silence, initially towards the silence between the notes, but finally towards the original silence. You can focus on the sound of the notes. When you're alert, you become aware of the silent space between them. When you become totally open, the preceding dimension of the great, stable silence opens itself. Music and silence come from there. That Silence is permanent, stable, strong and appears to be more inclusive than you could have ever imagined.

Schiermonnikoog, February 2, 2003

You've probably already experienced the non-dual coincidence of stillness and motion. When you are running really hard and fully concentrating just on running, it isn't always clear whether you're moving forward or not. How fast are you going?

Even if you start measuring, you see the relativity and elusive quality of speed. Physicists have always had great difficulties measuring speed. You can certainly say: speed is distance divided by time. Then you have the average speed, but not the speed of the current movement. If you want to measure the speed at a particular time, you can't do it. You can certainly make smaller and smaller trajectories based on the averages of so many kilometers per hour. Per minute, per second you still have only a trajectory, still only a traversed distance, and this distance you then divide by time. But still, you always have a trajectory in space and a trajectory in time. In a formula the trajectories can be made infinitesimally small and calculated (the sum of the limit in integral and differential calculus), but grasping motion in the here and now doesn't work, even though the here and now is the greatest reality. Here and now is the one place where we are present. In it you clearly confirm: here there is no movement. When you want to confirm motion, you have to start thinking that you have a trajectory again, that the here and now shifts and once again you take the average. But then you are making a mental construction! You can't catch movement in the here and now. Even though the here and now is reality. Do you see that movement as such is artificial? You take a measurement in the here and now at a specified time #1 and you take a measurement in the here and now at a specified time #2. What is the truth of that? That there has been movement in the time period from #1 to #2? No, because you haven't observed that. You have made two authentic observations; you can't say anything more. There was a perception from a state that was experienced as reality, then there was nothing, and finally there was (at a different time but certainly in the here and now) another creation. All connections that you make belong to thought structures. If you're honest, you can only confirm that there was a perceived creation at one time and a perceived creation at another time. It was always a new creation out of nothing, so to speak. Perception is always in the here and now. Motion is not there.

But watch out: there is no non-movement, either. When there is no current movement, there is also no non-movement. There is always the creation anew out of nothing, out of the silence, out of the non-duality. Thinking can also arise from there, also the thinking of movement. When you are searching for truth, you always need go to the source from which everything arises. Then the opposite of what you thought also appears to be true. Something is done; nothing is done. There is a movement; there is no movement. There is change, there is no change.

Scholastics ascribe this coexistence of opposites to God. They even try to prove the existence of God with it. If there is movement, then there must certainly be another movement that is its cause. So you can follow a long line of movements stretching back through time. But now which movement was the first? See the kind of crazy mind mazes you get? If you follow thought all the way through you come to the edge of thought. When you are consistent and think further, somewhere you see that thinking breaks open. If everything has a cause and every movement has a cause, then there must be a first cause. When an impulse arises somewhere for a movement, then again that impulse must also have another impulse as its cause. If you follow this infinitely you come to something like the Unmoved Mover, the Uncaused Cause, the Uncreated Creator. This was frequently a mind game. But here it has to do with your own being-experience of the highest reality. Thus when you begin to reflect, thought appears to become entangled at every turn. From an airplane you see the motionless waves of the ocean and from within you see that the plane is standing still. There is movement; there is no movement.

There is a stable openness previous to and beyond the opposites and also in relative space and time.

Is that clear?

When I walk, I've certainly had the experience that sometimes there is no movement.

When you walk and experience that you're not going forward, can you also still say that you have changed locations?

It happens simultaneously.

Yes, see how it is. When you say "there is movement", then you're positioned somewhere like a detached observer with a stopwatch measuring time and distance. When someone is moving exactly the same speed as you and you look at him, you will say "there is no movement". Both truths appear to exist simultaneously.

On the level of thought this means that you have seen through a fixed pattern. When you really let the relativity fully penetrate, you can get dizzy. You'll have to let go of thought. What's left over is the ineffable, non-dual. So you confirm that you are sitting here. You close your eyes, you open them again. In the meantime there is the emptiness. You wander on the beach. In one moment you are there – strongly, physically present. You blink your eyes, you see the immeasurably open space and in the next moment you're nowhere. Thought always takes up the old, doesn't see the emptiness and links the old onto the new. It imagines that your own identity and the identity of other things has remained the same. You say you know that the majority of atoms are quite stable, so matter remains the same. However, in experience everything is always totally new. You sit down to meditate: is there still time? Yes and no. Sometimes there is an actual perception of a clock and you confirm: Oh, a half hour has already gone. Was there really time? You say "time stood still". What do you mean by that? Actually, there was no time. There's only time when you mentally construct it. You point to the second hand. That's nonsense, because you only see the tick, tick, tick of the indicator. In meditation, there was no time. When you looked at the clock, there was. What's the truth?

I don't know.

When thinking breaks open in this way, what does it mean? All patterns of thought fall away. As soon as you say something, you will also have to say the opposite. "I see this, I do that" and "There is no 'I' that sees or does anything". There is a Zen koan which asks: What do you do when you can't do anything anymore, not even doing nothing? What is the solution to the koan?

I see everyone is thinking very hard…

In the great slippage
the words flow away.
The ability to form words,
deserts me.
A few patches still hang around,
scarcely word-memories.
The impulse to speak remains like
a stroke in the air.
The instrument has disappeared;
the intention ebbs away in
speechlessness
remaining
overwhelming silence.

4.2 Groundlessness and speechlessness

Gouda, May 22, 2002

[...] Stay with the Openness that is not limited by anything and goes right through everything.

What do you mean by "goes right through everything"?

Spatiality remains until the very last. If you want to speak about the non-dual openness in spatial terms, you have to say that the Openness knows no limits. In so far as it has a spatial character, it is not isolated from anything. It goes right through everything. Starting from the experience of a closed world, with boundaries at a specific location, there is the being-experience of the unlimited.

Although it's an experience of infinity, still you always have an experience and words which describe that experience.

Yes, up until the last it's a sort of spacious experience of being-self-being. And language can still be applied to it. It's one of the last things that you can still indicate using words. Also in large words like 'infinity' and 'spacelessness' the concept of space is still present. It's good to see how far you can go with language. In any case, when you are investigating this you are situated right at the outer edge. So try then, as well or as poorly as it may go, to describe everything. We are busy doing that, so that then – while you remain alert – the situation can really begin to turn around. Through words you can become more sensitive to it.

You can also see it this way: when you go with a certain terminology, for example 'the infinite', then at first it's just a word. When you really go into it, towards the meaning itself, the word quickly evaporates, while the inner meaning continues to manifest more and more clearly. It's as if it's a rocket-like motion. You see the night sky and use the word 'infinity' as a sort of goal. You experience an extremely strong impulse directed towards that goal – wham! You shoot into the air and are no longer standing on the ground intoning the word, like a beacon. There is just one focused impulse… and then you are in infinity. That's how it goes. That's also true with the highest mantra. When you are really busy with the mantra that refers to the highest, you get that rocket-like motion. As sound, as syllable, as word, you can sit down and have a good look at it. Then of course not much happens, at most your mind becomes a little bit calmer. But when you really let yourself go into the essential meaning… Then the words dissolve, then you dissolve.

Gouda, January 8, 2005

When words arise in the Inexpressible, the Inexpressible doesn't disappear. When thoughts arise, the Inconceivable doesn't disappear. Life goes on, but that which precedes life doesn't disappear. The creation doesn't destroy the uncreated. And, you yourself are That.

As self you precede every word, every thought, prior to life, prior to the creation. The forms that arise remain transparent and do not limit anything The sphere remains unrestricted. So we are sitting in the hall together and there is no one.

Is there anyone who has a question about any of this? [Silence]

Don't you see that no one is here, that there is an infinite inexpressibility?

Still I create my world once again.

Don't take creation personally. Of course there is a personal contribution to creation, but there is more to it than that. Take a good look. Often is it said very superficially: "The world is in your mind" and "You create your own world". That's nonsense. You don't create the world. You are too limited for that. It's too much for you. That's megalomania. What happens is that images arise, including your own self-experience. The images just arise in the great whole. It's all included there, including the 'I'-phenomena. Everything arises in the great sphere and in it everything disappears once again. That process is nameless. It has no creator. Where does creation come from; where does *māyā* come from? Nothing can be said about that, in any case the 'I' doesn't control creation.

You affirm that you are not different from this great, infinite space and everything that appears within it.

But attention for things always comes back.

Attention is a limited form of consciousness. When you go along with a special attention, you limit yourself as the open source of the attention. When you release that limited viewpoint then there is the unlimited being-awareness, the Inexpressible. It is there, but there is nothing that can be said about it.

That's happening now with the great natural disaster of the tsunami. People can certainly talk about it, but the disaster itself is inexpressible. All kinds of things have been said about it. It has been spoken about as a movement of the earth's crust and it has been said to be a punishment from God. But that talk is so limited. It is done from a limited viewpoint. The devastating effects of the tsunami allow people to experience that they are incredibly small, and that they are powerless. In relation to that natural disaster there is only speechlessness. In relation to the whole course of natural events there is speechlessness. The natural phenomena are just there, the whole process of creation, also of human culture. What more can be said? Only that the events are infinite and irreducible. It comes out of nothing, it has no solid ground. People who see it before their eyes stand speechless. If something is said, it's a mental construction that doesn't go to the heart of it. It remains irreducible to anything else.

People attempt to protect themselves from the inhuman space. They try with the assistance of technology and social controls to make a place in which it is pleasant to live. Then you hear: "We have arranged things pretty well here in the Netherlands." You see it: but then it only takes a report from the Pentagon to arrive with the news that in a few years the sea will extend to Amersfoort for those assumptions to disappear. The world may not be as solid as we might have thought. In Gouda, with twenty meters of soft peat underneath us, we are a bit more used to it, but sometimes you see the basic foundation of trust shifting to shock. You hear that from people who have experienced a significant earthquake. Then their trust is so deeply shaken that with each step they take, they ask if the ground they walk on is still firm.

You lie by the sea enjoying a wonderful winter vacation in the tropics. It is a matter-of-course luxury that Westerners can permit themselves. However, those assumptions are swept away by a wave that comes. Then the taking-it-for-granted-ness breaks wide open. Everything is so open that it can no longer be closed. Hence, there is speechlessness.

But certainly there is the instinctive will to live that continues.

That, too, is not personal. The personal 'I'-sphere of experience and speech has become irrelevant. Energies can certainly still function, but for you everything has fundamentally broken open.

Be clear about it and accept that breaking open. It is often said that after disasters the churches become flooded again. Why is that so? Because people are still trying to apply meaning to something that has nothing to do with meaning. Of course in the experience of the divine a greater realm arises than that of human technology and regulations, but the question is to what extent the openness remains. All too soon there are religious answers, but ultimately these are unsatisfactory. God, as the foundation of everything, is not completely knowable. Don't try to recreate a personal certainty towards that true openness, you can't do to it, you can't protect yourself. Just let everything remain truly open and allow yourself to be absorbed there in relaxation.

Soft energies arise
from original openness
just the glow
of infinite bliss
being without separation
in original openness.

4.3 "You are That": what is 'That'?

Gouda, December 6, 2006

In the approach of non-duality, self-being is usually the starting point as well as the pathway. Then the great consciousness or perceptiveness is frequently taken to be the endpoint. This approach can be found with a number of advaita teachers. However, for there to be real freedom, the last identification with that consciousness or 'I-am' will also need to be dissolved. For that the absolute must manifest itself and the non-duality with That must become clear. Thus, for the highest realization a definitive surrender needs to occur.

The most important passages (*mahâvâkya*) in the ancient Upanishads deal with the identity of the self and the foundation of the world, of Âtman and Brahman. There is the famous "You are That" in the Chândogya Upanishad. The title of the book of talks with Nisargadatta Maharaj, *I Am That*, indicates the same thing. The insight in "You are That" has not only to do with 'you', with self-being, but also with 'That'. The realization of the identical nature of 'Self and That' requires not only a clear being-experience of Self, but also of That. When that's not there, the liberating realization remains stuck at a relative level.

In our secularized world it's often not clear which experience has to do with That. What happens if That appears? Let's start with a closer look. When you are focused out towards the world and you see this and that, your living environment is quite closed. That's the case for most adults. There is a clear spatial structuring. Everything in the world has a clear geographical location. Also, in terms of time everything has a clear location, a place in the diary and on the calendar. Space and time form a relatively closed system: in perception, in imagination and thought, and in planning and memory. Everything immediately has a particular index in time and space. The same also holds true for other people: when you meet someone or think of someone, you place him or her within space and time. The same is also true of yourself. You have a self-image and self-knowledge, and this projected and known self gives you a constant position in space and time as a cohesive whole. Through this come all the additional conditions of the experienced world. One is causality, the fixed relationship of cause and effect between forms in time. Everything has its cause in a closed determinism. Another aspect is the identity of the things which persist through time: the things we have experienced as hard in the sense of material hardness and to which we have given a name (tree, table, chair). The world as a system of these fundamental structures (space, time, causality, identity, etc.) is well and truly closed.

Nevertheless the system is not completely closed...

[Suddenly the sound of a mobile phone; everyone looks startled.] You notice that. Suddenly something unexpected happens. Stay aware of what happened. First there was a shock. Now the unexpected is categorized once again as: "Oh, it's a mobile phone." But look again at the moment when the sound first came. In the unexpected even the orientation in space and time fell away, every definition fell away. There was just an open void. This actually happens quite often, the closed situation is broken open by something unexpected. You're shocked and your conditioning, mediated by the standard structures, just isn't there. Naturally the mind quickly categorizes the unexpected back into place, because it can't deal with something that's outside of its realm. Something happens that you can't place, that you can't reduce to the known. There is an infinite, absolute emptiness. You get shivers and goose bumps. Then you take an increasingly precise look. You search for the location, identity and cause of the strange happening. As soon as you find something that fits, the strange is changed into the familiar, the ordinary. The old natural order is restored and peace returns.

Last evening I went into a Turkish shop and wanted to buy some tea.

The shopkeeper said that he had just made some and asked if I wanted a cup. That was very nice. I didn't expect that.

Yes, that's the unexpected. How was that first fraction of a second when the unexpected appeared? Right then there is a disruption to your thinking because you didn't expect it. There is an emptiness. Then also there is embarrassment. Then, there is acceptance.

It came over me as pure love.

The acceptance created space and in this case it was a positive space, a space of love and goodness. There was no framing in of a certain bias, such as: "Turks are good for nothing." Every judgment closes you off, so nothing new can come. Now it stays open there and a dimension of unexpected goodness arises. When you accept the emptiness, when you really let yourself and your world open up through such an event, everything remains open, everything remains infinitely open.

In life there are always things that you can't categorize. You can become more aware of that. Then you must really take notice of it, because before you know it you have reconstructed the strange into something familiar. Then you're looking again at something familiar. The opening in the world is closed once again; the depth gives way to flatness. Sometimes you see through the surface of things. Then they take on a dimension of depth. That can happen with people with whom you have a good connection. In that deep contact you don't stop at the visual image of the other, the external, but you go beyond it. That happens already in every conversation that you have with another person. When you speak to someone, you're focused on the other as a person. Who is that person that you're focused on? It's not the external; it's not the whole of all the images or information that you have about the other. Information is not everything, even though today many people think so. The other has a depth of the infinite. When you have an eye for it, there is a perspective of infinity in the other. In your speech you are directed to the core of the person. When you ask someone something, you expect to get an authentic answer, that is, from their original depth, and not a programmed response from a robot. The infinite depth can suddenly come upon you and unexpectedly you are overcome, for example when you really look at someone. When you can accept the other with their unfathomable gaze, it can truly open. This can also happen with other living beings, animals and plants, and non-living things. They all have a uniqueness and depth that's just not compressible into your own fixed patterns. You don't create everything yourself. The construction of the mind is limited. The world is not a closed creation of the mind, but infinitely open in all directions.

Then amazement remains: how is it possible that forms come forth out of the deep-realm. What kind of realm is it? It doesn't fit into the standard categories of space and time. Additionally, through the content of your conversations with others you often go beyond material forms and towards life and experiences in all different kinds of worlds. Within this past, present and future come together; here and there are no longer separated. This also applies to looking at a painting, or when listening to music. Where do all these worlds come from? Where do all these forms come from? You stand amazed before simple things, a glass of water, a flower, the sun, and you suddenly marvel at the things that are there. When you don't directly insert the perceived things into the knowledge that you've already learned, then the things arise from an open sphere and you marvel. It's a miracle that these things exist. This also applies to your own physical existence. It's a miracle when you don't fall back into the obvious pattern. Everyday life shows openness in many places. Sometimes the openness suddenly breaks through.

I experienced that when my mother died. Her life passed away, but there came a large spaciousness of light. It was infinitely tender and good. I flowed into it. There were no separations any more, however much I resisted initially.

Why was it suddenly possible?

I think that my resistance had vanished.

Yes, with resistance you close yourself off out of fear of an attack and you create a judgment, so that everything remains fixed. The experience of becoming open is joyful. Stay aware of it and let the process of opening continue.

You see that death cannot be categorized. If, for example, you try and say, "All men must die," you've said nothing about real death. This meets you as you face the end of your own existence. You cannot rationalize it away, because within it is something that you cannot categorize. Death goes beyond time, space, causality, existence and non-existence. You get to know that sphere very well when you are in a situation of being overpowered, when you can no longer keep everything under control. Your order is disrupted, gets out of hand, and you have to surrender yourself to the un-organized, to the open.

That opening can also be very clear even when less drastic events occur. It's not dependent on conditions. When you have come to know the open dimension, you know: it's always there. You only create a world that is more or less closed, because you find it more comfortable and less threatening. You try to fit everything into it, but never quite succeed. We have seen that so far with the appearance of the unexpected, with perception of the deepest dimension, with amazement, and through confrontation with the uncontrollable, death.

Take a look at the situations in which a great fear arises. For example, a tsunami comes, and you have no chance to avoid it. In that fear a realm opens up which goes beyond the standard time and space of your everyday life. There is a contraction of yourself before something much greater, that is absolute and before which it's impossible to continue to exist as an individual. Of course there is the tendency to close that opening back up, to neutralize the terror. What are people currently afraid of: terrorists, a robbery, decay and disease. You only have to look at what they haven't already done to ward these things off.

Still there is a fascination for situations which inspire fear. People watch horror films invoking a high level of terror, for example, in which things suddenly appear and begin murdering. These things, organisms or spirits don't appear to be susceptible to control by people. But, it shouldn't become too tense or too terrifying. Then the film rolls merrily on. The familiar world closes back in again. People are always testing out borders, because what lies beyond the limits fascinates them – until it becomes too dangerous. Then they scramble back. Only through conscious surrender to the infinite greatness that opens up in the fear does all fear disappear.

Our sons have a fascination with horror. Is it necessary for their development?

It can work out alright, if they consciously get to know the structure of opening and closing, and the opening of the horror-dimension can come to be accepted within the relaxation of self-being. So for them it's about insight: when their own openness is allowed to remain, then the resistance to openness disappears and so too the problems of isolation. With isolation they can have a real problem and rightly so. They search out limits and the area beyond the limits. When it's really open, horror is no longer necessary as an expansion of the individual sphere and so normally it's no longer a problem.

Another opening in the everyday world is that of concepts. Through their knowledge people are constantly focused on what lies beyond sensory reality. When you see a cat, you see more than color spots on your retina. The visual impressions coincide with the concept 'cat'. But no one has ever seen the concept 'cat'. You only see cats, but you know that they are cats, because you have a general understanding of what a cat is. That one feline is expressed in the many concrete cats. So there is one life in all living beings, one gold in all golden objects, the same basic energy in all energies and in all matter. In modern physics there is a zero-field of energy as the foundation of all forms of energy and matter. We have a sense of the one that precedes time and space, the original. That original, which is also the basis of all that is, can be found in the oldest literature. From ancient times onwards it appears as a common human notion. In India it was referred to as Brahman.

Also, from the experience of good conduct, for example, that of a Turkish shopkeeper, a pathway runs towards Brahman. You see very clearly: this is a good man. No one has really seen this concept, yet you use it. The good manifests itself through forms. We take it for granted that we look through the sense-experienced world to the supersensible and then say: this is good and that is bad. We have within ourselves knowledge of both good and evil and recognize it in the world. Goodness, therefore, is not dependent upon a special situation. You can focus upon the good, so that it can be seen more clearly as such. It is an insightful beholding that goes beyond the externals of the sensibly perceivable surface. When you focus very strongly, the good becomes clearer, just by staying focused upon it. It moves increasingly into the foreground; it becomes the greatest truth. When you surrender to it there's only an ocean of pure goodness without limits, without time and space. How far does that participating vision go? Isn't it infinite? It goes beyond the sphere of time and space, beyond the opposites of good and evil. It has to do with something that is undivided and the foundation of everything.

Thus, the world as you experience it has an infinite depth. It can therefore break open into the absolute. It's important that you recognize that. Starting from the "me against the world" I can experience something in the world that doesn't fit into that category, which breaks that world open. Martin Buber speaks about historical periods in which mankind constructed a beautiful house using a particular worldview. These periods alternated with other times in which the roof of the house was blown off, or even in which the house itself was obliterated. Then you stand on the plain in infinite emptiness. Then of course people attempt to rebuild their house to protect themselves, but ever since the Middle Ages it hasn't really succeeded. People continue to hold on to the feeling of emptiness, even though they may relate to that void in different ways: by filling, forgetting or accepting it. There is no real ground to build on anymore. There is groundlessness.

Thoughts and feelings don't stop before a boundary. When a limit is experienced or suspected – death, or the end of the world – thought always asks what comes next. The only thing you can do is remain fully open. Then the tension of reconstructing boundaries disappears and real openness arises.

Usually it was the super-sensible which was the object of religious ideas and practices. During the last centuries, stories about God as the creator and ruler have been increasingly recognized as human and therefore relative projections. So too, the universal knowledge of God and his unconditional election (predestination) has been unmasked as a human projection. In Judaism, Christianity and Islam there's also a notion of the absolute (unconditioned) nature of God: no picture may be made of him, because any image is insufficient. In Hinduism people are not so strict; nevertheless there too, the in-conceivable absolute remains as the highest.

Thus far we have spoken about the nature of the world and the cosmos. At the same time it was also a talk about ourselves. Good is recognized, because it is already present within us. Love is recognized, because it is already present within us. This also applies to infinity. That which is beyond time and space, we can know in a special way, apparently because it is already present within ourselves. Everyone has a notion of the non-dual openness. We recognize it in the depths of another or in the world, because it is already present within us. It belongs to our self-being. To the extent that we recognize it in another, we recognize ourselves and so too the non-duality.

When everything breaks open and you let it happen, the self-being also breaks open. The two sides of your existence-world, subject and object, come together. When the infinite manifests itself on the object-side, it also reveals itself in you. When it becomes fully open there, your self-being also becomes completely open. The one condition is that you accept the opening up of the cosmos and self-being, which is to say that you release your limited form up to and including the 'I am'. Only through a complete surrender to That, does the realization arise 'I am That'.

Do you experience the deepest level of others, the other and yourself, even in everyday life? On which level are you primarily engaged? On the surface, on a deeper level of meaning which you recognize, or has everything broken so open that you are internally aware of the inexpressible? Then there are no separations. Self and That, I and Thou no longer form a duality. Therefore nothing can be said positively about it. Daily life may continue, but it has such transparency that the non-dual openness remains prominent as the greatest reality. You are this openness and it is not different from the ordinary things of life.

Lightning flashes from above;
the bright light strikes home,
consuming all
that is not light.
Thunderbolts tear open
the walls of the 'I';
only what is open
can maintain itself.

4.4 Religion and advaita

Gouda, end of 2002

Why should you trouble yourself with religion? Advaita goes further than religious forms. In fact, it precedes them. The best and only thing you can do is to stay with your intuitive sense of the great non-dual openness and don't let yourself be distracted. Still it's good, sooner or later, to acquaint yourself very precisely with the possibilities and limitations of the religious experience within your own sphere.

The core of the advaita approach is self-knowledge: a living insight into what you are not and what you are. A prerequisite for this knowledge is a clear view and recognition of everything that presents itself. This includes phenomena in the religious sphere.

What is the religious sphere? Take a look at the many forms. All cultures at all times create forms that we call religious: buildings, objects, rituals, texts, clothing, behavior and so on. These also have an 'inner side', that of experience, of belief. But what a colorful diversity. Nevertheless, they all have something in common otherwise we wouldn't call them religion.

All external and internal religions come from people who have a notion of the limitation of their own existence. You can't control everything in your own life; your living environment is small and your life is short. But this understanding of finitude presupposes a sense of a wider sphere in which these restrictions don't apply. When you have an experience or an idea of a boundary, it means that you experience yourself as within that boundary to the same extent that you know there is something lying beyond it. Religion is the relationship of men towards that which lies beyond the boundary of the normal human world, that which is transcendent in relation to this world. Many people find this relationship to be one of the most fundamental and intimate of their lives.

The transcendent is introduced in various forms and with

different names. There are supernatural phenomena and natural forces, superhuman beings, and omnipotent or omniscient persons. They have partly human characteristics, such as jealousy and anger, and are only partially subject to human limitations, such as mortality. The world of god (heaven, *devaloka*) is usually described as a place where there is no sorrow, where men enjoy everything that is desired here on earth: unlimited light, love, space, time.

You can just experience that you are now included in this light, this beauty, this softness, this heavenly song, where everything is only good. It's blissful, wonderful, more beautiful than words can express. You need never return; the world pales in comparison.

But heaven can also be here on earth, at least sometimes. Then there is peace on earth to men upon whom His favor rests. God or the divine also functions in different ways in the world according to religious experience or conviction. Such words as revelation, creation, providence, grace, or judgment refer to this kind of action.

The structure of the religious experience frequently illustrates a separation between the human and God, the divine. This duality is posited particularly clearly in the monotheistic Judaism, Christianity and Islam, although in Christianity one single exception is made for Jesus Christ. The separation means that there is a differentiation, whereby man feels himself small, sinful and inadequate. The Transcendent inspires reverence, trembling, and sometimes fear. Religion then is the whole set of activities performed so as to be in a good relation towards the Transcendental: devotion, worship, asceticism, purification, complying with the Law, etc. By developing a good relation towards the divine prosperity, peace, a blessed sphere and blissfulness can come.

When speaking of religious mysticism there is also a distance posited between man and God, but a distance which is to be bridged. There is a pathway towards union or towards a recognition of union with the transcendent. An idea that is logically connected with this is that the essence of the human and the divine is not wholly other. This is evident in non-Western cultures where a sharp division is not made between the human world and the divine. There are innumerable transitional forms such as demigods (man-god and god-man). There are also transitions through a divine incarnation or absorption into the divine world.

In the Vedic period in India there arose the concept of Brahman as that which precedes and goes beyond all forms. Brahman is present as the essence and foundation in all things and all beings, but which is nevertheless independent of them. In the Upanishads, didactic lines follow from daily things to the gods and the cosmos. Cosmic energy is an example. Then it is said that Brahman lies beyond and precedes the gods, the cosmos and the cosmic energy. This transcendent Brahman is the Reality that supports and enables everything. It permeates everything and so is immanent in the cosmos. It stays independent thereof, because it precedes and will also remain so when our cosmos has disappeared. Beginning then from the ancient Upanishads (8th century BC) it was said: "Thou art That". The infinity of the absolute which you discover when you penetrate to the foundation of the cosmos is also to be found in yourself. Self-study and self-meditation facilitate this discovery. That which you intuitively experience as Brahman outside yourself, you recognize as your Self. Both are identical.

For those who see the advaita approach as useful, it's good to recognize religious experiences and phenomena in your own sphere of experience and in relation to your own limits and possibilities.

1) To a certain extent, religion means a breaking open of the complacent me-sphere, the central focus of 'I' (egocentrism) and of mankind (anthropocentrism). Something from outside

manifests itself, making the 'I'-existence relative. A more spacious sphere is experienced. That is the value of religion.

2) Recognizing the religious aspects of your existence makes it possible to see to what extent you are stuck in limited religious ideas, how much the ideas limit your self-being. This extends to the level of subtle emotions even to those of your childhood such as dependency, determination and guilt. The conditioning of the child often plays a great role.

3) Sooner or later people on the advaita approach have a sense or an experience of That which goes beyond the limits of the human and the humanly divine. This notion is frequently missing and so also the depth necessary for a truly enlightening breakthrough is also missing. In the tradition, the requirement that the advaita teacher sets for a new pupil is that he or she knows the distinction between the temporal and the eternal. In the advaita path of self-examination and self-knowledge there is an ongoing recognition of that which you are in the unfathomable, deepest dimension of yourself preceding and beyond all self-images. Therefore, the openness of this dimension has a mystical-religious nature.

4) What is effective in the liberating breakthrough is the Openness. This manifests itself and makes the limited forms of 'I' and the 'I-world' radically dissolve. It is an action from outside. 'I' cannot liberate myself from myself. By yourself you can only remain open to the manifestation of the openness, leaving open a hole in the 'I'-sphere. Then there is the possibility of total dissolution, of complete surrender.

5) In the advaita realization there are no knots and restrictions any more on the religious level. That is not to say that the religious is gone, but rather that the sphere has fully blossomed. Transcendence has been fully realized, so that there are no real contradictions and divisions any more between the absolute, the divine and the human. In advaita, everything, even the religious, has come to a full development, since all restrictions have fallen

away. Only in the openness can life and world flourish fully.

4.5 Radical religion

Article: "Radical humanism – radical religion", in Nieuwe Stemmen [New Voices], 89 Number 2 (2006), pp. 26–32

From the beginning of liberal Protestantism in the 17th century, humanism and religion had a difficult relationship with one another. Yet those who formed the Free Congregation in Amsterdam (Vrije Gemeente) in the 19th century wanted to combine the two. At the time, P. H. Hugenholtz described it as: "Free of dogmas, free to critically choose from all major religions, philosophies and other sources of inspiration and insight, that is the Free Religion of religious humanism. Humanism yes, because with this our equipment consists of the human faculties of head and heart, reason and empathy, compassion and intuition, instead of unverifiable revelations" [in: *Nieuwe Stemmen* 88 (2005) Number 3, p. 7]. Through a process of demythologizing the Christian religion has gone beyond, and now the same holds true for the thinking regarding man. The question is what remains of religion and humanism, and what does that relationship look like. My thesis is that they both receive increased significance through this demythologizing and that they coincide when they stay true to their most central focus and intrinsic development. That's why I speak about a radical humanism and a radical religion (radix = root). I'll explain this assertion, beginning with religion.

Religion – the transcendent

In definitions of religion there are two elements which always come to the fore: 1) mankind with his focus and his answer towards 2) that which he experiences as a sacred reality and/or what he regards as the cause and controller of life. In any case this reality is partly transcendent to the human sphere. Rudolf Otto's description of the transcendent as that which is experienced by men is well known. It is the sacred which is terrifying, majestic and mysterious. Christians see the Bible as a book in which the transcendent reveals itself (for example, "I am the Lord your God") and in which rules are written for required conduct (for example, the Ten Commandments). Then it prescribes a particular set of behaviors for their relation towards the sacred.

The demythologizing of religion

From the beginning of the modern age (say 1600) there has been a movement in which the meaning of religion increasingly disappeared from life. The nineteenth century yielded Feuerbach, Freud and psychologism: the religious is a human projection. The biblical stories and representations are human through and through. They arise from certain forms of human interpretation. Human images, notions and concepts are projected onto something which is thought of as transcendent to human reality. Since the forties of the previous century, even devout Christian theologians from Bultmann to Kuitert themselves participated in this demythologizing. The stories of the New Testament contain a pre-scientific mythology that is alien for us and can now disappear. The criticism went so far that little of the transcendent remained.

Radical religion

In Christian thought there was and is a further growth in awareness of the cultural and general human factors in its worship service and through that a purification of these constructions and projections. It is seen with increasing clarity that the meaning of religion doesn't lie there. The transcendent can disappear along with it, but that doesn't have to happen. When the religious experience is purified (as much as possible) of human projections, the transcendent remains present as an open dimension. Every visual description is an inadequate human activity. That is the essence of the iconoclastic ban on creating any graven image of God in Judaism and Islam. A radical religion perseveres in this demythologizing. It lets all image forming activity fall away, or sees through it in its relativity so that it becomes and remains transparent. Through the disappearance of restrictive representations and concepts, the space that was traditionally seen as transcendent becomes open. It is no longer encased within ideas and concepts. It is groundless. The Kena Upanishad states: (*De elf grote Upanishaden. Tekst and toelichting*, D. Tiemersma, editor , publisher Advaita Centrum, Gouda 2004, pp. 117, 119)

> The eye does not go there,
> neither speech nor mind.
> We do not know That, we do not know
> how we can teach That to others. (1.3)
> It is not understood by those who understand;
> it is understood by those who do not understand. (2.3)

There is a notion of That about which nothing can be said. That cannot be filled in with images and concepts. That is openness. However, That is not a positive emptiness, because then it would stand in contrast to fullness. If you call it Emptiness, you must also say Fullness, the foundation of all forms. That precedes this opposition and absorbs both in non-duality.

[For the continuation see § 5.5 *Radical Humanism*]

4.6 The transcendent

From various introductions and talks

The experience of the transcendent

People are open to the transcendent, that which lies beyond the limits of their own existence. The transcendent can be found through the possibilities that exist just outside your own living-sphere and become feasible through travelling or through learning and exercising. With each learning experience your own world expands with elements that were previously beyond your field of vision. Through travel, old boundaries are transcended by crossing over into what was initially foreign territory. Hazardous journeys are undertaken to make the inaccessibly foreign your own. A part of what was strange and transcendent in other cultures comes to exist within your own horizon. Limits are consistently sought and surpassed because the transcendent fascinates and attracts. But the transcendent always remains, despite the crossing of boundaries. It appears to have a depth that is not bridged by a limited self. How can the limited completely break through its own limits?

The experience of the ungraspable transcendent is also available within the realm of knowing. New possibilities of knowing and investigating using new perspectives present themselves, so that new territories come into view. What remains is the recognition that reality cannot be completely encompassed by human knowledge. Something new shows itself, a strange area opens up in your everyday world and it's immediately clear that your own knowledge falls short when trying to place it into the familiar context of an image or formula. This is particularly clear when life suddenly loses its meaning or with the prospect of your own demise. Then a hole exists in reality that cannot be plugged, a white spot that you cannot color. Such a hole or spot may present itself so intensely that it manifests as an endless depth. The blind trust in your own knowledge disappears and reality breaks open definitively. That openness has a tendency to overwhelm.

This also happens with real amazement, when suddenly a dimension of the mysterious breaks through into everyday life. You see a flower and suddenly experience the unknown strangeness of its existence with all its forms and colors. What is the source of its origin? How is it possible that it exists? With respect to the known an estrangement has occurred. Suddenly something familiar becomes very strange. This means that a dimension of depth opens which can no longer be closed. The strange can also suddenly appear: the ungraspable cosmic space of the starry sky, the inhuman forces of nature, or the complete strangeness in the way someone approaches you.

That strangeness, that otherness, can so intensify in experience that it sweeps away all familiarity. This happens especially when it's clear that the forces of the unknown are uncontrollable, that you can't control everything as you might wish. Great natural forces such as a tsunami, the force of someone else in a surprise attack, or actions of groups that are unreasonable and not susceptible to countermeasures. These unknown and uncontrollable forces are portrayed in films and literature, simultaneously displaying the vulnerability and desperation of human beings. They touch upon a sense of uncertainty and the feeling for the transcendent which people appear to have. The transcendent dimension also opens in the state of fear.

In various aspects of life there is regular contact with the Great but without the element of fear. In going to sleep at night there is a sinking into the inexpressible. When you have a feeling for the depth of the dreamless sleep, there's a sense of it. And in the morning upon awakening, a notion of the large open space without content is present. It's wonderful to let that continue, when you can afford to lie there just a little bit longer. Then there is a joy that has nothing to do with objects and duality. During moments of the day when there are no thoughts, when the mental images and thoughts fall quiet, there is an emptiness that doesn't have a place in time. When these moments become clearly conscious, there is the realization that the void is always present as the foundation of the world with its many forms. Everyone knows something about this. There is a fundamental openness in all people for that which transcends the human condition. Specific forms of spirituality then can be more of a temporary interest or whim. The openness of existence is a given with human consciousness.

Thinking about the transcendent

The transcendent also arises in thought, even though it cannot be fully contemplated. It arises when thinking pushes itself to the very edge of its own possibilities. What is the cause of this phenomenon and what is the cause of that cause, and so on. Eventually you come to the question of the very first cause. But this progressive regression appears to be infinite. This endlessness cannot be fully contemplated. Many texts from the Indian tradition concern themselves with this dilemma. In religious Hinduism, a personal God (*Ishvara, Brahma*) is indicated as the creator of all. The advaita tradition calls this God-creator Brahman with properties (*saguna Brahman),* but the one source and ground of everything is Brahman without properties (*nirguna Brahman*). It is unknowable, nevertheless we have a sense of it. The medieval proofs of God also stem from this notion. Although they are in the form of logical proofs placed within a conceptual framework, they refer to That which precedes and goes beyond the framework: the uncaused Cause, the unmoved Mover, and so forth.

Thus the transcendent has in principle a dimension that we cannot know, but of which nevertheless we do have a notion. Concepts and ideas go beyond the limits of the strictly sensory perceivable phenomena. Concepts are thoughts existing upon a mental level (*manas*). Ideas that are direct and go beyond have to do with insight (*buddhi*). Certain ideas have to do with pure qualities which lie beyond all conceptual opposites and finally are so refined that they merge into the openness about which nothing positive can be said any longer.

'Essential' is such an idea. In the many sits one essence: the space inside of the pots and the houses is one; the gold in all golden objects is one, and so forth until: the being of all beings (all that is) is one. There is this and there is that, but everything has 'being' in common. In ancient India that That was called Brahman. Through knowing Brahman, the essence, the being-ground or the self of all, one knows all. So too, the self of yourself: that is Brahman in you. Brahman is truly beyond positive being, because it is also non-being. It includes this possibility. It transcends the antithesis of being-non-being. It is immanent, positive, but also permanently transcendent, indeterminate. A concrete insight of this is possible.

There is also the idea of immutability, even though all sensory perceivable events and psychological phenomena constantly change. These changes are in relation to previous, also changeable conditions, but are also in relation to the unchangeable. The very idea of change has within itself the idea of the unchanging. The idea of the temporal goes together with the idea of the non-temporal. Even if it's possible to think of everything as always changing, through its continuous change its changing remains the unchangeable. Everything constantly moves on, while there is no movement. There is a notion that the ultimate emanates from beyond change and positive immutability.

This is also true for the idea of emptiness. Positive emptiness is still just an aspect of experience, when the fullness of the world disappears. Real emptiness goes beyond the opposites of emptiness and fullness.

The idea of goodness also arises when you meet someone in

whom you experience only goodness. This benevolence goes beyond any action that the person performs. You experience a depth of goodness. The experience is a resonance in yourself of your own goodness. You become gentler in relation to others. As that process continues, the goodness in your own sphere becomes increasingly lucid and purified, which is to say increasingly independent of your own 'I' and your own circumstances. There is an increasingly confident feeling-experience of what true goodness really is. You can mentally project yourself there in that direction, so that you enter more and more into the sphere of pure goodness (Plato). This Goodness expresses itself in a natural way in all behavior, because the whole being-sphere is that of goodness.

The action of the transcendent

In open awareness before the infinite, the transcendent can manifest itself as something great that comes at you. Then there is an experience like an attack, an attack against which you can't defend yourself. It's an enormous physical power that overwhelms you, a cosmic force that washes you away. The force can also take the form of a judgment. You are viewed from an infinite perspective, you become objectified, your limited 'I' is destroyed.

The open transcendent can also have a sucking effect because of its emptiness. The emptiness is a vacuum, an incredibly strong underpressure in which everything disappears, everything dissolves. With such an underpressure everything immediately evaporates, including solid matter (sublimation). No material or energetic form can stand up to it. The dissolving effect of the great is too strong.

What happens to you varies as the overpowering continues. Is your consciousness strong enough to remain aware while your form disappears? Then it can happen very quickly. The Great can be like a needle that punctures the balloon of your ego. In a moment you burst apart.

Everything that you grasp onto will disappear. When you grasp onto the perishable, there is suffering. If you grasp onto it with all your might and stay identified with it, the suffering is enormous. It concerns your own existence, even though you know that this existence is finite. When you don't consciously experience that you are the emptiness, you remain tied to what is not empty, with of all its consequences.

There is also the possibility of recognizing the infinite as your own the being-sphere (see Chapter 5). When the recognition is not complete, there is attachment and a desire to hold onto the form. The identity that exists with that form can then be released through surrender and trust. When that's the case, it seems to just happen. You can't really control it yourself. If it does happen, there's the sense that it's grace.

When you already know your own self-being as boundless, you no longer have to hold on tightly to your limited form. In the true recognition of your own nature as openness you have already released the limitations of your existence. Then you have already gone into that great openness which invites you. You enter into That which initially seemed infinitely transcendent, but now appears to be the very core of your own self-being. That is the radical non-duality of the deepest self-being and world-ground that is both transcendent of and immanent in the world (see Chapter 6).

from out of nothing
a tingling
an eruption
an unexpectedly intense
electromagnetic field
light from a thousand suns
just light
luminous atoms

the northern lights
a cosmic shiver
to darkened forms
of a hard world
a cosmic laugh
a melting
a fusion
in light
preceding every tingling
from out of nothing…

5

Self-being as groundless openness and non-duality with the external openness

An inquiry into the nature of self-being reveals that there is a depth and height to the detached witness-consciousness and the universal consciousness and bliss-being. Ultimately, self-being appears to be nothing more than groundless openness. In that, it is not different from the external openness.

At the extreme edges of existence
– just try it: you find it in every direction –
name and form disappear.

Also in the direction of self,
on the edge of center,
nameless depth and formless void appear.

I am this empty depth,
the core of being, at home without name or form,
an outpouring of love without borders.

5.1 What is radical self-inquiry?

Gouda, January 6, 1999

If you want to get to know yourself better, it's useful to see what this learning consists of. Self-knowledge arises when you are aware of yourself in your situation, of your actions and reactions to all areas of your existence. An inquiry into yourself is a systematic and critical activity. With a radical self-inquiry, this continues through into the core of your existence. What does this consist of? The difference between it and an ordinary inquiry or examination is clear. In an ordinary examination a difference exists between yourself as the examiner and that which you examine. For example, when you examine a patient, a soil sample or the market, you are careful to influence the area in question as little as possible. The ideal of scientific research is to make this separation complete. To examine yourself is a strange proposition, because the examiner and the object of the examination are the same: you are both. It's worth taking a closer look at several aspects of this phenomenon.

1) Every investigation begins with an idea of what you want to investigate. In this case, it is the notion of yourself. Everyone has such a notion, evident just by saying; "I did that" and "I'm going outside". Every use of the word 'I' presupposes the knowledge of your own 'I', your own self. When we began this evening by sitting quietly, there was an inward return to that self-being. The strangeness of self-inquiry lies with the unfamiliarity you experience in relation to that which is so well known, with what is nearest to you: yourself. Apparently you don't have a complete knowledge of yourself. If you did, then there wouldn't be a need for self-inquiry. The map you have of yourself contains vague and blank spots. The most important cause of this is the fact that you are usually focused outwards on things in the external world. That is also true for this investigation. When you see, hear, act, you don't have much attention for the organs and psychic processes that are involved in these activities. To the extent that these are the means of your investigation, they are not an object of it. For example, you may look with your eyes but you don't see your own eyes. When you are viewing something in the world you forget yourself. The means with which you see has no form. Most certainly there remains an ego-function which concerns itself with everything regarding you as a person, but this is seldom present consciously. Then there is no notice taken of the additional contribution of the 'I' to the perceiving and the

perceived phenomena, nor to your reactions to these partially self-constructed phenomena. So there remains a more or less closed circle of constructions and reactions to these constructions, a self-made cage. Pessimists see only the darker side of the world and become confirmed in that view. Fearful people see snakes on the ground everywhere. Aggressive people meet only people against whom they have to be very aggressive. Usually the lack of awareness of this situation is not so serious, but when you look a little further you see what kind of unpleasant consequences it has. It creates tensions, conflicts, suffering, not only for you but also for others. These consequences of the ignorance of your own situation are often the starting point for self-inquiry.

Thus, at the start of an inquiry there exists (a) a notion of yourself, that (b) is not entirely clear, but which (c) through inquiry you expect can at least become clearer.

These three points remain salient throughout the entire investigation, albeit in various forms. Just see if this is true in your own experience. Continually check these statements and then, when they are acceptable, try to see as precisely as possible what they mean.

2) Through inquiry a surer clarification can indeed arise, the knowledge of yourself can grow. The inquiry can take place from a detached viewpoint through observation of the physical forms of your body. For example, the biological examination of anatomy, physiology and genetics, together with the observation of behavior, offers many details which lead to a greater self-knowledge. But you are also that which perceives these details and expresses them. Therefore this information is not everything that you can come to know about yourself. From a more or less detached viewpoint you can perceive additional private phenomena about yourself, such as your bodily impressions, feelings and psychic processes. By pursuing this path you can learn a lot about yourself, for example your way of reacting to other people. But here too, you can't get a complete view of

yourself. You have the notion that you are more.

So there is a certain clarification possible of aspects of yourself, of a public and private nature, with which you are identified to a greater or lesser degree. To the extent that you, through your self-inquiry, understand, confirm and express these phenomena, the identification with them is no longer so evident. At the same time, the clarification seems to not have gone far enough.

3) You will have to formulate more precisely what it means that you confirm details about yourself, that you are the one who carries out the self-inquiry. With this investigation you take a distance from yourself in order to see yourself more clearly, to become aware of yourself internally. Apparently you are self-reflexive, which is to say, self reflecting, and in this situation something of yourself becomes visible and expressible. We call this reflecting situation consciousness. We say: "I am conscious of myself," which is to say, I have a way of being that is characterized by the reflection of myself, my being is a being-awareness of myself, an aware-presence-being in which I see something of myself. In the inquiry, this being-awareness can extend itself so that more and more details about yourself come into view.

This being-awareness of yourself can appear in different degrees of clarity and is a prerequisite for the possibility of self-inquiry and self-knowledge.

4) As being-awareness you experience a certain freedom in life and society. As long as you are aware of a situation, you can talk about it, think of alternatives and perhaps do something about it. You are not completely subject to a fixed situation; you aren't caught in a closed circle. The factors acting upon you are not all direct. There is a space in which you can act, in which you can interpret, think and speak. This space gives you a certain freedom from your situation. Being-awareness, then, is the first-person aspect of this space, or the light in which something (third-person) appears before you, as first-person.

When the consciousness is reflexive such as in self-inquiry, there is a certain freedom of being-awareness with respect to aspects of yourself that were initially experienced as data, a freedom from your identification with these circumstances. The clearer the awareness, the greater the possible freedom.

5) The process by which you come to know yourself better and become freer through a clearer and more expansive awareness can develop in different ways. A few ways, which can also be combined, are the following:

a) You can withdraw to an ever higher point of being-awareness, through which your manner of being changes. Your identification with the phenomena that arise in consciousness, such as the properties of your body and images of yourself, can continually diminish with respect to an increasingly spacious and less differentiated being-awareness-being. This is one of the main threads of Advaita Vedanta.

b) The direct insight can grow that the phenomena, such as feelings and thoughts which belong to your identity, have no over-arching 'I', which is to say that the 'I' identity increasingly disappears. This is one of the key elements of the Buddhist path.

c) A third option is that your attention for your current situation continues to open, which is to say, you become more open, more sensitive to others, released from your me-centered 'I'-structures, with a positive acceptance of everything and everyone as an extension of yourself. The inquiry then concerns your own boundaries. Wherever you look, they don't seem to exist.

d) This insight is also present in the direct submergence of your aware being in your self-being. Initially you noticed it as an unclear feeling or vague premonition. Then it seems that self-being is actually an unlimited and undifferentiated self-consciousness.

With every path of self-inquiry, a change of insight also means a change in your own way of being. Knowledge and being go together in your own being-awareness. In this realm, a greater insight (being-

awareness) immediately means a manner of being that is freer in relation to previously unconscious identifications.

6) The radicality of self-inquiry means continuing this investigation as far as possible. The insight grows, you change, you become increasingly self-aware and you enter into a transitional area, where something else will happen that is no longer covered by the inquiry, that no longer belongs to the realm of "I am doing self-inquiry". This is an event that comes from the outside. It overwhelms you, there is a surrender. It is an event that is direct, without planning or mediation, even though the additional experience can be from Another or from something cosmic. It is a sea of being, consciousness and bliss, within which every limited identity falls away.

Thus, radical self-inquiry leads to a point where an insight into unlimited-being can break through. This also corresponds to the liberation from every limiting 'I'-aspect. It is the end of the inquiry, the end of every definition through words. It is the end of the 'I'-self. It is the insight which understands that the belief in all those limitations was an illusion, the insight that you always already were yourSelf, the unobjectifiable background from which everything arises, the openness.

7) In the liberated 'situation' the 'I'-self and inquiry no longer have a role to play. To the extent that they still manifest within people, they are strictly relative, namely involved in the human situation of self and inquiry. They are then regional phenomena appearing in the openness, while the openness itself is not limited by these phenomena. This also applies to the words that may still be used, the different words from the different traditions, which refer to the openness. An inquiry conducted under differing circumstances (such as hatha yoga and meditation) is generally useful, as is the study of expressions of authentic experiences, in order to come closer to the transitional area of the openness in experience. For this investigation then methods do exist, but these concern only the preparation for the actual realization. The disappearance of borders is a direct event

through the insight "There are no borders". In the real insight there is an openness for everything and everyone, for all aspects of life. With it life is totally changed, as long as it goes on.

The inquiry continues to be valuable then within a particular arena. In the open-being-awareness everyone and everything can be accepted without talk of any restriction whatsoever.

8) The above is an example of a description of self-inquiry. Every reader can do the same investigation. Take your time, otherwise there is a great chance of jumping past important phenomena. Remember that it is a living insight and not a theoretical one. Carefully stay with each step and check to see that the formulation still makes sense. When there are clear differences within your own experience, then suggest alternatives or additions. Then there is something to talk about. Yet it is remarkable that relative to the important points there is still a high degree of correlation between the different traditions.

I've lost myself
in the sea and wind
only the rustling
still remains

I've lost myself
in the infinite murmur
only as rustling
do I remain

but that rustling gets forgotten, too
in luminous openness
appearing sometimes as
the rustle of
sea and wind

5.2 Insight into the difference between the one who sees and what is seen (Drig-drishya-viveka)

Stoutenburg, October 10, 1998

The following text is a record of the first introduction and talk from a retreat weekend. The starting point was the Drig-drishya-viveka, a short text of 46 verses, in which an important part of the Advaita Vedanta teaching has been assembled. Another name given to this treatise is Vākya-sudhā: the nectar-words, or translated differently: the essence of the instruction. Under this name it is attributed to Shankarācārya (Shankara, ca. 750), but it's more likely that it is by Bhārati Tīrtha, the 14th century Jagadguru from the Shringeri monastery founded by Shankara.

The purpose of the instructions in the Drig-drishya-viveka is the breakthrough of insight into the nature of yourself. As the name of the texts suggests, this occurs by seeing through the difference between the perceiver and the perceived. Through this there occurs an awakening in the core of your own seeing, free from every objective conditioning. The version from Swāmī Nikhilānanda (edition Ramakrishna Ashram, Mysore 1970) was used for this English translation from the Sanskrit.

We've come together this weekend in order to gain greater clarity into the nature of ourselves. This consists in seeing through all sorts of restricting concepts about ourselves and releasing them as illusions, in recognizing quite clearly that your Self is not limited by any form or concept. When this insight breaks through it is called 'enlightenment'. We begin with one of the classic texts in which the core of this wisdom can be found, this wisdom which emerges again and again at different times and in different places. We call it a classic text, because it is has been handed down through the centuries and is discussed anew, again and again. The text has shown itself to be well worth the trouble of discourse.

Investigation

The title of this text is Drig-drishya-viveka. 'Viveka' is the distinction that you make in order to see things more clearly, the investigation in which you set all sorts of things apart so that you can identify them: this is not this, but that. It is an analysis. 'Vi' means apart. 'Viveka' also means the capacity to distinguish, the discriminating insight that you apply in order to know what's what. It is this sense of *viveka* that we will use for examining ourselves. Because of this you have to consistently confirm for yourself what there is to confirm. From a certain perspective you see this and as you take the next step you see that. That's the beauty of the tradition of insight yoga: that you see what's what for yourself step by step. It is obvious that you can only do this in an alert way. When you sit there and doze off you learn nothing. When you remain alert, you receive the guarantee in advance that you will finally see whatever there is to see. With full attention you go forward step by step and finally affirm: this is it. You must clearly see the situation in every phase so that you'll never forget it. Don't skip steps, because then you'll find that you are somewhere without knowing where, and with a great probability that you'll have to start all over again. Always look very precisely at how everything happens. If something isn't clear yet, take another look. You take the next step only when it's clear.

This valuable guided investigation as a path towards liberation is characteristic to a large degree of the yoga tradition that has proved successful throughout the centuries. Of course you do find paths to liberating wisdom outside of this tradition, but hardly anywhere as detailed as this. Western Christianity primarily has to do with belief in things that one cannot see. There is certainly an appeal made to your own insight and your own orientation, but this is too vague for most people, grounded too little in the development of their own experience. In the book *Science of the Soul* (by Swami Yogeshwarananda Saraswati), there is a program of yoga that guarantees enlightenment in three, or for mediocre students, five years. That's nonsense, because the final and most important phase of the path is no longer a path. Then something else comes into play. Still some part of that assertion is certainly true, when you are very rigorous, and go about your work very consistently, step by step. But most people don't do that. So what happens primarily depends on you. Yoga has to do with a discriminating investigation on all levels, including bodily yoga. Consistently confirm: I perform an asana (posture) and this experience is associated with it. When you perform the same asana again, there is the same experience. Then you confirm this clearly and you gain knowledge of the posture thereby, what it means, what effect it has on you. This also happens with jnana (insight) yoga: you get insight through positioning yourself in a particular way and seeing what there is to see. You name it and then you know it clearly. It is often difficult to put experiences into words, to capture them in language. Do this as long as it is possible to do so without losing the essence of the experience, because it creates clarity. This applies also to when you read something: after reading it you affirm it for yourself, you verify. For each examination determine what your starting point and method is. Then you can come to know exactly which results come from which methods. You need to be extremely sharp.

A special aspect of self-inquiry is the fact that you, through a greater self-knowledge, change into something that you already were. On the one side you change and on the other side you remain the same. What changes is your method of knowing and thereby your view of yourself changes. It concerns an expansion of consciousness of yourself. That's why in the Advaita tradition they say that actually there is nothing to be done, while on the other hand instructions are given through which you can change your way of being. It's about realizing the situation as it is. Through that insight you receive an instant realization (it becomes reality) of what was already there. It is a realization for you because you have realized it. This is possible due to the nature of yourself.

The starting point

Self-inquiry is a process of becoming aware of your own situation. In the Drig-drishya-viveka it's about becoming aware of yourself as the one who sees something. What can you say about that seeing? Who or what truly sees now? This question can already be found in the Kena Upanishad (*kena* means: 'by whom'; from *De elf grote Upanishaden* [The Eleven Great Upanishads], op. cit., p. 117).

1. Impelled by whom does the mind proceed to its objects?
   Commanded by whom does the first life-breath move forward on its path?
   Prompted by whom is this word that men speak?
   What god set eye and ear forth to their workings?
2. That which is the Hearing of our hearing, the Mind of our mind,
   the Speech of our speech, it too is the Life of our life-breath and the Sight of our sight...

It's about that which makes hearing, thinking, speaking, and so forth possible; it has to do with their source. It's a backwards questioning in a backwards motion. The backwards motion means making yourself free from the physical eye, ear and so forth.

The explanation from a physiologist about perception is different. Then that's about the rays of light which are broken up in the eyes and create an image on the retina; it's about impulses from the eye to the primary sensory cortex in the brain and onto the secondary association centers. That's all. He doesn't have the total picture regarding vision, only about physiological, material processes. What happens in the physiological view only takes stock of the material terrain. It's a materialistic theory.

It's important to take some distance from this and other theories that you may have learned. When you take these theories with you into your investigation you block seeing reality. So go back to your own experience. In it you notice that seeing is direct. You see something or you don't see it, period. An image arises and disappears again. So you can also direct your attention toward the process of perceiving and see precisely what it contains. How is it with seeing? In any case your body has something to do with it. You can close your eyes and the visual world outside disappears. You press a little bit on your eyeballs and the visual world becomes deformed. It's clear that the seeing of things has something to do with the eye. This was also stated at the beginning of our text.

Drig-drishya-viveka

1a: Form is perceived and the eye is its perceiver...

But what is the eye in your direct experience? For you to become aware of this direct bodily experience it's good to look once again at your approach, to the nature of your attention. In seeing, you normally have your attention on things in your surroundings; the point of attention is there on the things. Then you can bring this point of attention back to yourself. Try out this little exercise. Hold the fingertips of one hand next to each other in front of you and direct your attention onto them. You see your fingers there, your point of attention is there on your fingertips. The place in yourself from where you see your fingers is somewhere in your head, behind your eyes. You can verify that there is a distance between the point of attention on your fingers and yourself. The point of attention comes closer as you bring your fingers closer to you. When you close your eyes, the point of attention stays there with your fingers. Open your eyes again and slowly bring your fingers with the point of attention on them closer to a location on your forehead between your eyes. So then it's more about a mental attention than a sensory visual one. Do this motion a few times so that you know precisely what it's like to shift the focus of attention, though already it's no longer the focus of your external gaze. Now let the focus of attention go from outside to inside. Take care that you don't have any tension in your attention. The attention must stay open and relaxed. Once inside your head you can observe anew what there is to be observed.

The eye

With your attention inside your head you experience many impressions and feelings. At the location where your eyes exist you experience something, especially if you roll your eyes around in their sockets. You perceive your physical eyes there at that particular location. The question is: where is the perceiver? It's about how to determine that now. In any case the perceiver is not located in your eyes, because you experience your eyes to be at a distance from yourself. It's the same situation as it was earlier with the seeing of your fingertips. Is that clear?

Yes, that's right. I experience that I'm not located in my eyes and yet I perceive.

You perceive your eyes. You confirm that there is a feeling in the area of your eyes. This perception happens with your inner sight at a distance from your eyes. I had a friend once with a glass eye. He would take it out now and again when he wanted to make a point… The eye is an external form, a thing on which you can fix your attention. It's there then, before you, you see it. You can talk about it. You can describe it. How does your eye feel? Burning, tense, stinging? As you move your eyes around in your eye sockets you can feel the movement. These are all observations of yourself. You are focused on your eye. The conclusion from this piece of investigation is that in any case, you as perceiver do not reside in your eyes. At best the eye is an instrument which makes a contribution towards establishing a certain type of observation. The eye is not the perceiver. The perceiver is found even closer to you. Is the brain then the perceiver? Many contemporary philosophers, psychologists and neurobiologists maintain that the mind is an aspect of the brain's functioning or is identical to it. But like the eyes, the brain is a material structure and the processes are material processes, which are perceived from a distance. The brain and the brain processes too seem not to be the perceiver. The real perceiver is not a brain process. You could say that it takes place in the mind.

Drig-drishya-viveka

1a: Form is perceived and the eye is its perceiver. It [the eye] is perceived and the mind is its perceiver.

The mind

What is the situation now with the mind and all of its activities? We say that perception and thinking take place in the mind. Let's take a precise look at what is happening there. For this it's necessary to go further within, to withdraw further. Switch your perspective backwards, so that you can look back at the field of your mind.

With the perception of a tree a visual image emerges. It's a certain form that arises in the mind. It's a representation of something in the external world, about which you can think and over which you can speak with others, even when you are somewhere else and don't see the tree any more. The actual image of the tree can be very sharp or quite vague. The properties of the image also depend upon your previous experiences and your current knowledge. When you no longer focus on the tree there in the garden, but on the image of the tree in your mind's eye, the image is a thing with properties that you can discuss. So the entire mental world has properties that you can determine. Early in the morning you say half sleepily that your mind is not yet entirely clear. If you have to think clearly you experience a mental dullness. You concentrate yourself upon the thought formations in your mind. Your mind then is a totality of mental processes with which you function.

Now does perceiving take place in the mind? Many psychologists who deal with imaging say: yes. On the mental level you can at least determine that a transition has occurred from the material world to something that you label as your mind. The area of examination is altered thereby. But now you must examine the new situation. There is an image of a tree, a certain depiction, a certain representation. You perceive this; it is again a situation of perception. The image is an object, on which you've directed your attention. There is a distance between that object and yourself as perceiver. As perceiver you have shifted backwards. And that's how you see images with all different kinds of qualities in your mind. Usually your approach isn't such so that you have an overview of your mental field. But if you situate yourself in this way you can keep looking at the whole world of your mind. Then you can have all kinds of beautiful images spontaneously. You can look at memories that arise and then disappear again. Sometimes there are fantasy images, creative images. You look at them and see that the world of images is a spectacle, a world of objects that you look at. This mental world of objects is not the perceiving self.

Drig-drishya-viveka

1b: The mind with its changes is perceived and verily the Witness is the perceiver.

The return journey

With the return to yourself you experience once again the same situation that we have already spoken about on different levels. From a distance you see the field in which the forms are present and you say: "I see everything there." It is an always renewed backwards step and a review. Then you notice that you see more and more. It can be compared to climbing a mountain. You ascend the slope of a mountain and regularly stop to look back. It's a beautiful panorama that continues to expand. The higher you climb the wider the landscape becomes and the more you see. That's also the case here.

In addition to seeing more there is also the following aspect. As you ascend higher up the mountain you release all sorts of things that occupied you in the valley, things that you were involved with. You see something of the busy mess below in the distance and realize that you've let go of it. When you return below from the elevated heights you get caught up in the world once again. Thus there is something special happening there in the changing of your perspective. What is special is that you throw yourself into each world as you go towards it. You identify yourself with all sorts of things in the world. The entry point is a kind of boundary between yourself, what you are, and what you are not. The border of yourself can completely descend, so that you identify yourself with the things there. This also happens with your body. You incorporate (embody) or incarnate (become flesh) yourself, whenever you return to your body after you have withdrawn. From a distance you saw the physical body there before you. You can take distance once again and through that step the identification disappears, the incarnation too. At first you sit in your eyes viewing things, but by taking a step backwards you see your eyes from a distance. Whenever you see your body from a distance, you are not situated in it. If you step back even further you see the entire mental world before you. Seeing, itself, doesn't take place through the means of these phenomena.

Stay aware of the steps that you take: first this, then that. Be aware of what happens the moment that you see something in front of you. At first your boundary is somewhat withdrawn. In that situation you experience a reincarnation by going into the body and completely involving yourself with it. It is a common human process, the continual shifting of your boundaries. You find this always and everywhere in your own situation. When you have a lens, you're not analytical about it, but instead are busy viewing other things and other people. You have incarnated into the lens. It belongs to the bodily sphere from which you see the world. That's also true for the clothes you wear. It applies to your belongings; it applies to your home. In all of your property there is a quality of 'me'. This means that you have gone further into the world and incorporated yourself into it. Conversely there is often a withdrawal, too. "Well, I was really attached to it but now he can have it." You take distance from what at first belonged to you and you do that by repositioning your boundaries. When you were young and played with marbles, the marbles were really important. It wasn't good if you lost any of them. Adults also say if they lose something that they are attached to: "That was dear to my heart." But the release really happens. The marbles aren't that important anymore. You can look at them from an objective distance. It's always about the borders that are there between myself and another person or another thing. The borders shift constantly and that's something universal. That's also one of the most fundamental processes concerning social-political events in the world. For example, consider the Balkan people. There's always an identity of a people, with their traditions and land, while throughout history these traditions and residential areas significantly shift and change. The identification with your body is very strong when you're healthy, when you can easily do everything required in the world. Only when there are problems with your body is your attention directed to it. "Ouch! That splinter is deep in my finger," and your finger becomes a thing at a distance from which you can extract that splinter. When you get an injection the nurse objectifies your arm and that's a good thing. Otherwise she couldn't give you the injection. When you have to inject yourself, you shift the border backwards and then you can inject something that is hardly yourself any more. Your boundaries shift constantly.

When you inquire about yourself, you quickly come up against a phenomenon and ask yourself: what is the situation now with myself as perceiver? The eye isn't the perceiver, because there is a distance between myself and the eye. By going further backwards it becomes clear: the mental processes are also not the perceiver, because there is a distance between myself and the psychic processes. Then it's time to ask the question once again: what is the situation with the real perceiver?

The witness

From the position where you observe the thought processes you are once again going to withdraw the point of attention. This happens in the same way as when you let the attention that was on your fingertips come inside your head, in the direction of yourself as perceiver. From the mental field, too, you can very specifically withdraw your attention back to yourself as the one who sees. What about yourself as an observer on this level? What can you still say about yourself when you perceive the mental processes with all their various forms? In any case you are consciously present, you, as being-awareness, are present. You have a viewpoint from which you see the mental processes, the body and the world, but there is no clear form of an 'I' present. This lack of a clear form arises because you have let go of many aspects of your body and mind.

When you are situated physically in the world, you are mostly involved with what you see. When there is something wrong with your body, your attention is not only focused on it, but also internally connected to it. You are your body and therefore whatever happens to your body happens to you. When you are involved in an accident you are totally connected to it. The report that you give afterwards, you give from your involved position. The police will also want to hear a report from someone who was not directly involved, because that person can give a more objective report. If someone happened to be at the scene, he describes everything that happened, but remains neutral. That then is the witness, who gives the police information about what happened. The witness is present at the event and records it without being involved. When you are involved in the world and in your body, you don't have an overview of the events that take place within your own situation. You see everything but from a limited perspective. When you take distance, you have a 360° view of your old position and can report much more objectively about what happened and is happening there. You come to the viewpoint of the witness when you inquire about yourself as the true observer. It is not to be found in the mind, because the psychic processes form the object of perception for yourself as witness. The actual perceiving doesn't take place there, but rather here on your own side of perceiving.

Perhaps it's good to go back to the text again and re-read the entire first verse.

Drig-drishya-viveka

1. Form is perceived and the eye is its perceiver. It [the eye] is perceived and the mind is its perceiver. The mind with its changes is perceived and verily the Witness is the perceiver. But It [the Witness] is not perceived.

We will return to discuss the Witness in a moment. But now there is a special phenomenon to be noted which we haven't discussed yet in the movement towards the Witness: on every level you begin from a large quantity of forms that you see, but which come together in you as observer.

The object of perception is multifaceted. It consists of many components and features, while you as perceiver are one. It is the many, which is the object to that which is the one. The many are absorbed into the one. In your visual field you have to deal with many different forms and properties of the things that you observe. They come together in yourself, but what you are appears to shift. What comes into view, and thus becomes a new object, appears to be a complex multiplicity, which is once again absorbed into the one perceiver.

Drig-drishya-viveka

2. Forms appear to be various due to such distinctions as blue, yellow, gross, subtle, short, long, etc. The eye, on the other hand, sees them, itself remaining one and the same.
3. The mind is able to cognize characteristics of the eye such as blindness, sharpness or dullness, because it is a unity. This also applies to the ear, skin, etc.
4. Consciousness illumines desire, determination and doubt, belief and non-belief, constancy and its opposite, modesty, understanding, fear and others, because it [consciousness] is a unity.
5. This consciousness neither rises nor sets. It does not increase; nor does it suffer decay. Being self-luminous, it illumineseverything else without any other aid.

It is only in this consciousness that perceiving occurs.

5.3 The witness (sâkshin)

Gouda, November 5, 1997

The consciousness-space

Tonight we will look at the different states of consciousness. It will become clear that it's important to gain a better knowledge of them, to clearly see what the situation is of your own consciousness. To begin with it's good to look at the most common form of consciousness. That is the form you experience during the day, when you are busy with all sorts of things. You look out towards things while you are busy with your work. A consciousness is there, because you can speak about these things. You know what's going on, you see it and you can interpret it somewhat, you can place it in relation to all sorts of other things. From the viewpoint of yourself there is a certain consciousness-space, where you are positioned on one side and on the other side are the things towards which you direct your attention. You are directed outwards somewhere, you have your point of attention there, as a focus of consciousness. The consciousness-space is located between yourself and that focal point. In this space you see many things, you notice everything, you can be active in this space. This situation of your consciousness-space is usually present: the space can be large, but can also be limited, it can be vivid, but can also be dull, you can be awake, but also sleepy.

Self consciousness

You can also expand your consciousness space, expanding behind you, in front of you, expanding to the left and to the right, above and below. Especially when you expand into the space behind you, you experience something very remarkable. At a certain moment you experience a situation in which you are aware of your bodily self in the world. Under certain circumstances people can experience this kind of awareness on a continuous basis. When you need to be aware of your balance, you must be very aware of the horizontal floor and the vertical axis of your body. This is especially true when it's difficult to maintain your balance. For example, when you walk across a beam or when you perform certain balancing exercises in yoga. The function of these exercises is to have you become so aware of your body that you clearly see what its position is with respect to the horizontal ground. When you are no longer aware of your body in space, you fall. What happens with your consciousness in each of these situations? That's what this is all about. Another example is the following. At a given moment, everyone has certainly had the experience of looking at themselves through the eyes of another person. Small children experience this when they get the idea, "Hey, I'm a person just like everyone else." Then there arises a somewhat more objective picture of themselves and the world. Sometimes it disappears a little, but now and then you have that experience very clearly. You can see yourself anew through the eyes of someone else, you see yourself in your situation. It's about seeing what kind of consciousness this is, what kind of properties this consciousness has in respect to the most common form of consciousness that we have just spoken about.

Distance and reduced involvement with the seeing

It's clear that there is a certain distance. You take a certain distance in relation to yourself. This distance can be larger or smaller, but there is a distance because there is an increase in awareness, a seeing of yourself in space. You become aware of the whole situation in which you find yourself as a physical human being. As this distance increases, you receive an additional aspect along with that, which is that your degree of involvement with the situation decreases. The greater the distance, the less your involvement. You see everything at a distance, not only that you have a greater distance in the space, but also in relation to your connectedness, the importance you feel about a particular situation, your interest in that situation. When you take a large enough distance, everything becomes a picture more or less in which you're no longer involved, where you no longer need to bend everything to your own will, to control and so forth. A third point, after distance and the reduced involvement, is seeing. From a distance you see what happens and what is present with less involvement. We have already seen that with walking on a balance beam, when you also take account of yourself in space you are much more aware of your own situation than when you are completely immersed in your body and identified with it. Only when you take distance do you get a good picture of your situation. Thus, concerning this form of consciousness, there is a greater space. There is greater distance, with much less involvement. Consciousness is much less involved in the situation. It is a clear seeing of what's going on.

Two forms of yourself as consciousness

How is it now with yourself, because apparently something has happened there. Apparently, at first there is an 'I' or self in the world, an empirical 'I' that lives, acts, experiences, perceives, that strives to achieve all sorts of things. This covers all aspects of the person as we usually understand him: the physical-material, psychological and social aspects. You function physically in the world in these ways. Of course there is a consciousness, but that is a consciousness which is directly linked to the 'I' in the world. Then there is the detached self. Suddenly you see it all before you: that empirical consciousness completely involved in the world. There, all affairs are important, all kinds of things are desired, there are ideas, perceptions, actions. And then there is the self that sees everything, without involvement. There is a seeing, but it is an aloof seeing, an observing, from a freer perspective, just as someone who sees a house as he walks past it: he is indifferent to it. He perceives it and can possibly look at it with extra attention: "This is like this and that is like that." Whatever is said, it is a perception as a confirmation, nothing more. That's the idea of the witness, of a witnessing of something without being involved in it. When there is an accident, people want a witness, not someone who was actually involved but who was in the neighborhood and certainly saw it. When you hear the story from people who were involved, you get a completely different account than from the people who witnessed it but were not involved. The story from the latter is much more objective than from the former. Thus you have two forms of yourself as consciousness. In the old Upanishads you have stories and images that describe them. For example, in the Mundaka Upanishad there is the image of two birds in a tree. One bird is eating fruit from the tree and is actively engaged; the other is on a higher branch and does nothing. This one only looks at what the other one is doing. There are two forms of consciousness. The one completely involved, the other who sees it from a distance. The important point is that this is the normal situation for every human being.

The discernment

It is a matter of recognition to see the witness, of getting to know it in a conscious way. When you take some distance and are able to see yourself, it's clear that on the one hand you have an empirical self and on the other hand a self with a quality that is even more essentially you. You see the empirical self and say: "Yes of course, in a sense I am that." On the other hand you confirm: "No, I'm not that, because now I am the self that sees, now I am the observer; now I am aware of what's happening there." You are dealing with an 'I' as subject that sees and with the bodily situation which you see as an object. So there is a separation between subject and object. While you are in the situation, you don't make this separation. Then subject and object are completely intertwined. When they are pulled apart, only then do you see the distinction. Then you can determine who you really are. In a certain sense, I am that 'I' there, living in this body in the world; in a certain sense I am bodily present there, yet I feel that only the witness is my real true self. All the perceived qualities can change, everything can fall away, and still there is the idea of the ongoing self. The recognition of that witnessing self arises in the first place by making the distinction: "I am not this, but that."

The evidence of consciousness

The witness-self is something that is self-illuminating. It comes out of itself, completely from itself. All things in the world, including your body and your psychic functions, are only visible through consciousness. They arise in the space of consciousness, become clear, and are visible. When something is observed there, then an observer is necessary, an aware-being. In that sense the observed is not independent, but rather is dependent upon consciousness. Is that also true for the self of the conscious-awareness, does that also require something? Traditionally it is said, it shines by itself, it manifests itself. It requires nothing more than itself to manifest. That self-consciousness is there. You don't have to do anything for it and nothing extraneous is needed. It is the first fact that there is: self-being. It is also the most obvious thing there is, once you have recognized it. Everything in the world of phenomena is dependent upon something else, namely upon other things in the world and dependent upon the consciousness through which it can be present. In order to be known, a phenomenon is dependent on consciousness. Consciousness really cannot be known as an object, because you yourself are that. As self you are always present, even if you dive back into the world and forget it. Yet the consciousness principle is there, as a principle by which you can see something, by which you can become conscious of something, even if it is in a limited manner. On the one hand you have the world with all different kinds of phenomena, the innumerable aspects of the person in the world, the countless events, the multitude of things. On the other hand everything is absorbed in the unity of the aware self. Everything is absorbed into one unity and this unity is necessary to allow that multiplicity to appear. If this unity of consciousness was not there, how would you ever perceive anything? You always have the one, whereby the many can appear. Retreating from the many, you come to the unity of the conscious self. Again, this need not be proved, because everyone experiences this as the core of themselves. When you take notice of it, you confirm that this is the greatest truth that there is. You can doubt everything, but you cannot doubt yourself. Traditionally this is also said. The self arises and flourishes without needing anything. It is a light that shines from within itself and through which all forms become visible. The forms have no light of their own and must therefore come into the light in order to be made visible.

Being free of the empirical 'I'

As consciousness you look at everything and realize: these are wonderful things that appear here, but there is a definite distance. As self-being I have a relationship with them, but as self-awareness I also have nothing to do with them. It's clear that that brings a great freedom. It's a liberation from everything that at one time imprisoned you. At first you can see this as a transformation of your consciousness. It's a change from a very limited and fragmented consciousness, towards a totally open consciousness in which everything becomes visible. You can also see it as the transference of your point of view about yourself from in the world, to outwards, so that a completely different perspective arises. It's a becoming aware of a 'higher' self. This is always present, because otherwise you would have no idea of things in an objective sense. As I have already said: a child learns first of all to look at himself through the eyes of another, through the eyes of his parents. Only then does the child form a more objective idea of how the world works, that he is not the only one present in a world that is the only world. Then he sees in a less naive way that he too is a little person in this world, a person whom others also perceive. This creates a certain sense of self, an identity. This phase of personal identity is needed in order to let go of it in a conscious way. You can see the stages clearly and consciously confirm them.

It's important to always be aware of your witness-being, again and again. In any case, during a certain phase you'll have to practice, to take the perspective of the witness once again when you have gone back into the world. You will have to do this until you always take that position. To repeat, the witness is a matter of awareness, for it is always present. It is always the whole background of space, clarity, consciousness, which is necessary for becoming aware of anything at all in the world, even when you are fully in it. You can always talk about your own situation, as seen from a different viewpoint. This is a fundamental human capability: to be able time and again to be aware of your own situation. In principle, this is always the case. You can always say, "I did this and I did that." Animals can't do that, but humans can. Why? Because it's dependent on that witness-consciousness. You have an aspect through which you can reflect everything so that you can have knowledge about your person in the world. It is a mirror-function, a reflection. Literally, 'reflect' means to bend light back. We often say: "I need to reflect on that." This means that we want to think about something. But then you are on the level of thought. You can go further and reflect on that thinking without thinking, namely from clear consciousness. Therefore it is said that the witness is nothing more than a mirror. The mirror is passive, is not troubled by what it reflects. It remains clear and pure, no matter what is reflected in it. It is a consciousness, through which everything which appears can come to the fore. As an exercise it's good to take backward steps in a very practical way, so you can see yourself sitting, so you can become aware of yourself in the situation. It means that then you release yourself from your identification with your bodily viewpoint. It means a release of your identifications. You see it all. On the one hand you have a relationship with it; on the other hand, you have nothing to do with it. When it really works, the whole bodily state relaxes. Tensions aren't needed any more, because you no longer have to be concerned about them. You're no longer specifically involved in everything that the bodily person in the world wants or doesn't want to do. When you are no longer specifically involved, you're free. It also means a physical relaxation, because it's the bodily 'I' as an incarnated self who wants and doesn't want all sorts of things and that's tension. When you withdraw into yourself and can look at everything quietly, can reflect, can let everything relax, it's because the old 'I'-structure has loosened. The self becomes free, because there is no longer a limited 'I' that is causing tension. This has to happen in a very concrete way. You see yourself in the situation and you can let go of yourself and the situation, completely let go. Then you notice to your amazement that nevertheless everything continues on and in a very good way. When you have experienced something like this, it gives you confidence so that you can let go of everything. You can let everything totally go, the whole world including your own little person, and everything still continues on in a good way. The less you interfere with it, the better it goes. When you've experienced it once it gives you confidence, which makes it possible for the process to continue. Continue to let go. Do you see, everything goes great just by itself? So stay in the viewpoint of the witness in that great conscious space.

The insight body

When it really works for you to remain in the viewpoint of the witness there is one more point to consider. The self is self-consciousness in the space of consciousness. That self-consciousness doesn't really have any characteristics, except that it reflects, that it has a mirror-like aspect. Yet it has another characteristic, namely that it is localized somewhere in the great space. You are yourself somewhere and see everything from a certain perspective. You will frequently take this viewpoint so as to be able to touch base, in order to avoid falling back again into the old location in your body. When you are able to stay there a long time, you will become aware of your situation anew. As self-consciousness you have a place somewhere in the consciousness space, because you see everything from this location. Take a look once again: there is space left, space right, above and below, before and behind.

Apparently there is something present in the location of the witness that is physically and spatially localized. It is something taken from the properties of the body. One of the elements is the perspective of your body, the place from which you view everything. When you are at a different location you have a different perspective. Something of that physicality is carried into space, to the witness. The witness has a rarified physicality. This witness body is the body of insight. In the [Advaita] tradition it is called the insight-body. It has nothing to do with the mental and energetic world. It is a more rarefied body, which is to say that it has many less properties than that of the physical body. In that sense a purification has occurred. In that insight-body everything is very pure, because it has a mirror-like aspect. There is still an I-with-qualities, because there is a particular localization. You view everything from a certain position and there is space left and right, on all sides. You can be aware of that at the location of the witness.

Becoming free of the witness

At the location of the witness: you see everything, you are clearly aware of everything, you see your bodily situation in the world and are aware of the distance that is there. Imagine that you look down at the round ball of the earth from the great cosmic space and you see how busy you are. You see it and say: "So that's how it seems to be." You observe everything, confirm it and say: "I am myself, as one who sees everything, who observes, who reflects." Once again, you are positioned at a certain place looking at the earth and yourself. But, what about to the left and right of you? Become aware of your new situation in that big space, that great consciousness-space. Just turn yourself 90 degrees to the right. What happens then? Then turn yourself 180 degrees. If that would really happen, then what would you still be able to say? What would happen to the whole structure of the seer and the seen, to the structure of the witness-self and the All? What you can do is remain standing at the border, so that you can always become more aware of the situation there. Turn yourself around once again. Just take a step outwards. Then fly away. The final structure of subject and object, of the seer and the seen, disappears.

Is there really such a clear witness body from the beginning? I've noticed that when I try to take a distance from my normal stuff, I create a truer and more transparent viewpoint. Is that witness-body something that you created by yourself through time, or was it already there?

It has to do with the way in which the withdrawal takes place in consciousness. To a greater or lesser degree the qualities of the physical body come along with it. There remains only the localization, the particular spot from which you see everything, without qualities. When instruction is given about it, it often remains limited to the viewpoint of consciousness as a witness. To the question "Who are You?", it is answered: "You are consciousness." But keep looking further. Your true nature does not have any structure and quality. Living in the world, all levels of the self are present, consciously or unconsciously, including the corresponding bodies and the freedom from those bodies.

In the word 'consciousness' [tr: bewust-zijn] is the word 'being' [zijn]. Can you say something about this?

When it concerns the pure witness-being, there is, as I said, still some physicality remaining. It is awareness and being and even a localized being. You are present there. When that's released: there remains only pure Being, Consciousness and Bliss, all in a very pure form. These are the last things that can be expressed. You can't speak about the Ultimate. It is not Being, but also not Non-being.

What is it then?

Follow the advice that I have given to you: remain at the viewpoint of the witness, so that it becomes your own viewpoint; then turn around and fly away. Then you are not far from knowing.

5.4 Stories and patterns

Gouda, January 8, 2005

When you remain lucid and relaxed, you clearly experience becoming free of yourself. You confirm that spaciousness comes and you are freer.

What happens there happens at the expense of the story of your existence in the world.

That story can continue, but there's no bond anymore with the inside of that story. That applies to your own invented stories. It also applies to the great stories of authoritative others and also to the cosmic story of *māyā*. These stories may continue. You read a fairy tale book to children and tell stories. Children experience the creative effect of the fairy tale. They are absorbed into the fairy tale world and it's real. Adults see that and for them it's not so difficult to let the openness remain with respect to the little stories. "These are just fairy tales." But then someone else comes along and says: "You're this and that" and immediately you fall for that story. So you'll need to throw some light onto that process of intake and absorption. It is a story from another person. If they believe in it, it doesn't mean that it has to be yours. People become involved in each other's stories as reality. Especially sensitive people who can easily enter into it. Then it is said that the person is weak and that the 'I' needs to become stronger. That you should become more assertive with your own story, in response to another. That you mustn't be put off balance. That if you can maintain your own story, adjusted to your life, you'll become well again, declared normal. But, don't you see that your ego-story still remains and that the conflicts haven't disappeared from your world?

I have nothing to do with all these stories.

Then at least it remains wonderfully open. It's about the recognition of openness and freedom. That's the freedom from stories.

MRI – Gouda, August 2006

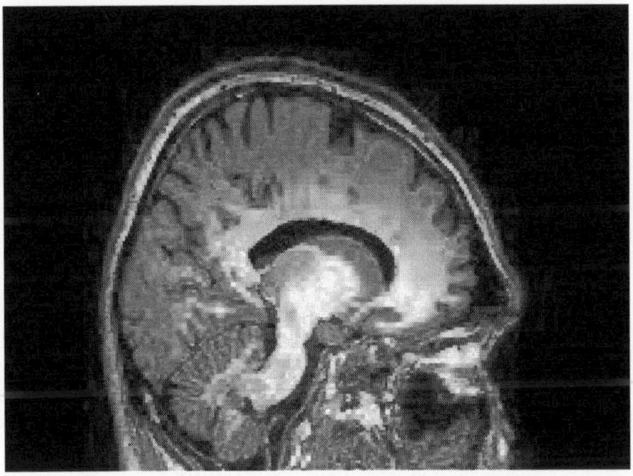

What am I? This question can lead to a deeper knowledge of self-being. At all different kinds of times and places this question arises, for instance when you receive a photo of an MRI-scan of your brain.

Am I that? No, of course not. I am not that photo. I am also not the grey mass of which this is a photo. I see this as first person and I am not an object. This would be true even if they needed to cut into that mass. Strange that I could hide myself in that mass, so that then they would be cutting into me. Fortunately that's not necessary. In experience, I am certainly connected to it everywhere, but that's without a particular location, precisely because I am not nor do I have a standpoint. In the unity without standpoint there is no one to whom the cutting could happen.

It's a miracle that sensory perceptions, feelings, images and thoughts are connected with the brain. Apparently the connection between the mental processes and the physical brain is a connection between object-phenomena which reveal themselves as subtler and coarser, respectively. So they belong to the same realm. I am consciousness.

I can completely dive into all these phenomena, but that's not necessary. Physical and mental things remain as objects for myself as consciousness and from there simultaneously they remain in an open manner as not different from myself. This non-dual coinciding is inexpressible.

Self-being as light – Gouda, October 29, 1980

Could you say something more about clarity? I still have trouble with that. I have a tendency to stay in the thinking mind.

Clarity doesn't come from the intellect, the 'mind', the thinking faculty. It is where perceiving and discrimination take place.

You can say quite a bit about perception: what happens in the senses and the nervous system, what psychological factors are at work there. But about perceiving itself you can't come to it from externals. Perception is something that falls outside of the scientific world. There is a consciousness principle which illumines everything, including that which science presents as knowledge. Without that light everything remains dark. Then there is no world and no body. Where can you find this light? Perceiving takes place 'in your innermost' space, in yourself. The perceiving itself is being-awareness, the consciousness that you are, as first person. As Light, you are before and beyond all substantive knowledge, including scientific. You, yourself, are the foundation of all knowledge and all things. As consciousness you are irreducible to anything else. There is nothing to say about that. It is a miracle that there is light. It's about perceiving that as Self-being. You will become more and more aware of it. Restrictions appear in the person through the nature of the senses, the brain and so on. You can say a lot about those forms. You can do that, because there is light. But about that light itself, nothing can be said. The source of light, as Self, you can only be.

Freedom from patterns – Gouda, August 2005

One of the elements of the retreat last week on the island was experimenting with the structures of perception and physical orientation. For example, what is horizontal?

Looking towards the horizon on the quiet beach, you only need to twist your head towards the right, and the horizon goes upwards to the right. If you let your head hang longer in this position, then on the right is the beach and the sea, on the left is the blue sky: the horizon is vertical. If you walk a little to the right, you seem to walk up a vertical wall. If you continue walking in the same direction, you'll notice that you walk around to the right and you end up back at the starting point: the space is curved.

Breaking through fixed structures brings freedom. When deep-seated structures of orientation are broken through, a great freedom is created. Sometimes there is dizziness at first, which is caused by holding onto the old orientation. When this is released, a great space is experienced on a deep physical level, on a deeper and more practical level than it's possible to experience with just a mental approach to advaita.

On Saturday, just after returning from the August retreat, I walked with my little grandson down the street. He walked bent forward with his head completely skewed. He enjoyed that. Nobody had taught that to him, but apparently children like to experiment with various forms of orientation and perception. This can also be found in your own childhood memories. Actually, that freedom from patterns is never completely gone. You only have to play games again and the open situation without a fixed position returns. Some on Schiermonnikoog [an island off the coast of the Netherlands where the retreat was held] said that they had become a child again. Wonderful. "Yes," I said, "but now it's aware, so that the freedom can always be there."

Portrait
Do you want to create a portrait?
What is there to portray?

The images in the mirror are myself as much as any other images;
self-image and body-image: constructions that erect nothing and everything.
Experience itself is empty and also full of all that is;
life is not divided into mine and yours;
portraits are mists;
descriptions are just a shot in the air;
biographies have a fictional duration.

Even the notion of a portrait of someone:
an inner contradiction, impossible.
The frame itself is already too much.

5.5 Radical humanism

Article in: Nieuwe Stemmen [New Voices] 89 Number 2 (2006), part II. The first part "Radical religion" is in § 4.5.

Humanism – the autonomous man

Humanism, such as that which developed in the 19th century, depended heavily upon the Enlightenment of the 18th century. The central point of the Enlightenment lay in the self reliance of the human being who used only his reason and intellect to gain knowledge and insight. The Enlightenment emerged from the darkness of religious dogmatism and from a type of faith which had not been based on science or reason. The Humanism of the 19th and 20th centuries linked to the Enlightenment and offered a view of man in which human rationality and autonomy were employed in contrast to religious faith and its dependency. Man is autonomous, which is to say not dependent upon God-given rules or laws, insofar as he uses his own rational capacity to achieve insight into moral values and the cosmos. He has no need of divine revelation for his theoretical and practical knowledge. In this respect reason assumed the role that God had played in medieval thinking.

The dethronement and disappearance of man

This rationalistic view of man became criticized in a manner similar to that of the religious concept of God. Romanticism emphasized the sensory and feeling aspects of knowledge. Especially in the 19th and 20th centuries there arose the strong sense that man and his knowledge were finite and limited. People are determined in both their knowledge and behavior by their biological construction (Darwin), their instincts (Schopenhauer, Freud), their social position (Marx), their conditioning (behaviorism), history (historicism), language (grammar, stories) and the media. In empirical research it became increasingly clear that many factors are involved which determine man's existence, including his knowledge. Thus, much damage was done to the rationalistic view of man. Over time, a large part of the humanistic movement incorporated this dethronement of reason. The feeling and intuitive aspects of human existence, and so also of knowing, were still recognized for the most part. However, the demythologization of this view of man has gone even further.

In the last decades of the 20th century, in what has been called postmodernism, the critique was pursued so far that there is hardly anything left of an image of man. The image destruction became complete. People are nothing more than nodes and the product of major networks such as language and media. Humanity understood anew Nietzsche's statement "God is dead", a God who guarantees the truth of our knowledge and the certainty of our moral principles. People had sought a replacement for divine authority in human reason, but this attempt lead to shipwreck when the conditioning of reason itself became clear. Foucault showed that after the death of God, 'man' was also doomed to disappear. 'Man' as a relatively recent conceptual creation now quickly fell away. Especially with the young generation, you can hardly see any of the great concepts or myths that are necessary for an image of 'man'. Life is a conglomeration of events in many areas and with many layers that have little consistency, lacking a significant image of what a human-being is. So, is humanism obsolete in this post-humanist time?

Radical humanism

The criticism of the rationalistic view of man was evidently correct. The rationalist's pretensions proved to be untenable in relation to the limitations and conditionings of human existence in the world. The postmodernist critique, in which very little of the idea of 'man' remains, also has a strong case. Just like religion, humanism did not escape demythologization. Thus the humanistic critique of religion continued on through to the critique of humanism itself. Still, there is more that can be said.

The humanistic point of departure, which is that we have nothing more than our own human cognitive powers as foundation for our knowledge, is unavoidable. Reason belongs to these capabilities, the reflective reason that animals don't have. Certainly reason is one great hallmark of man. In the 17th century, Pascal recognized that man is a fragile cognitive reed, but that man in his thinking also embraces the whole: "through thought I can embrace it." This awareness "to embrace everything" is present in man in an authentic way. Thus it is right that it is honored in philosophy and in the philosophy of life.

However, this comprehensive capacity of man was taken in too limited a sense; that is, only in relation to rationality, to which some thinkers added feeling and intuition. The "I feel", "I think" and "I see into" did not enter into this above-mentioned critique. To the extent that they are seen as something more than fleeting, the modalities of the 'I' in their conditions and assumptions are viewed as a myth. Does nothing remain of the human being, as the ideas and stories about him disappear?

What is present in rationalism and also what Pascal meant by comprehensiveness in the human being is the infinite dimension at the very core of the human being. This reflexivity of being-awareness continues on into infinity. This also applies to the feeling dimension: the feeling sphere knows no boundaries (see Romanticism). The self in its feeling aspect and being-awareness is infinitely large, larger even than the sphere of reason. The forms, through which all cognitive capacities display themselves, can be objectified; but for the first person, the self-being, this does not apply. A subject can never be an object. The criticism dissolves into the open dimension of pure subject. This irreducible dimension is present in all people. Sometimes it becomes quite clear in an encounter. Especially in the 'great teachers' such as Buddha and Jesus, but in principle in all the people you meet, there is an experience of infinite depth. This openness imparts both a particularity to each person as well as a similarity to all people. It is the condition which makes the mutual connection and communication between people possible and also forms the foundation of human rights.

A humanism? Yes, but a humanism without a rationalistic prejudice and with a serious grasp of the infinite height and depth of the human-being. In that infinitude lies the freedom of the self that humanism defended. It just thought too small about the human-being. A radical humanism goes back to the core of its intention and moves it forward to the most radical of consequences. Everyday life with all its conditioned assumptions continues to hold great riches, but it is not absolute.

Radical humanism and radical religion

It is clear that religion and humanism in their radical forms have much in common with one another.

In radical religion there is the notion or experience of the transcendent which stands free of human projections. The representations of the highest or original source become either transparent or disappear altogether in favor of letting the infinite dimension open. In radical humanism there is the realization of human independence and freedom which goes beyond conditioning and objectifiable forms into a groundless openness. That's the benefit of the demythologization in both areas.

The transcendent sphere is not separate from the human-being. Apparently there is an openness for this sphere within people. Apparently there is something in man himself that corresponds to it. That is the irreducible dimension within the individual self-being. Through reclaiming the conceptual projections of 'God' and 'Man', the transcendent and irreducible self-being appear to come together in a non-duality. In openness before the transcendent and infinite within himself, which exceeds the conditioned human-being, there is the being-experience of being one with that which was initially experienced as externally transcendent. The Chândogya Upanishad repeats it many times: You are That. There is no duality between the transcendent and the groundless immanent. Thus, humanism and religion coincide when they stay true to themselves and to their intrinsic development.

Here I am in the garden, nowhere else;
I am *now*, not yesterday, not tomorrow.
Here and now, I am.

I am here everywhere;
I am now always.
Here and now I am everywhere and always.

The here of everywhere is nowhere;
the now of always is never.
Here and now I am nowhere and never.

Here and now I am everywhere and nowhere;
here and now I am never and always.

5.6 The dissolution of the last standpoint

Gouda, December 7, 2005

When you really remain situated in the standpoint of the witness, you also feel the last residues of that constricted-being dissolving. Experience that very practically.

The standpoint of the witness is your last standpoint. Within it there are hardly any more personal elements. You are just a standpoint of being, of seeing, of the witness-being of phenomena. From yourself as witness there is still a perspective. The phenomena appear within that perspective. That is the situation in vipassana meditation: you are witness of the phenomena and there is a clear perspective.

At this point you can become aware of yourself anew, as witness-being-awareness, as the standpoint of consciousness from which you view phenomena. As you become aware of yourself there anew, the infinite space that surrounds you manifests itself. Then the final viewpoint automatically dissolves.

What does that dissolution mean? Take a look. Can you say anything about it? It's the dissolution of the specific perspective, but along with it also the dissolution of your standpoint. When there is no longer a perspective, then there is no perspective-construction of the visual field: a construction which contains a vanishing point in the infinite in which all lines converge and from which all lines return, to a vanishing point in the center of perceiving, in yourself. When this structure dissolves, what does that mean for you, for your own identity? As standpoint you dissolve. Thus, you dissolve. Take a look at what that means.

When things appear, it's from a certain perspective. If the null point of the perspective from a particular standpoint is released, then there is no preferential perspective any longer. Then there are an infinite number of perspectives. Then isn't your own perspective everywhere? When you see someone, you also immediately see his or her back side. You immediately see the way in which he or she sees the world. Also you are the other. The true releasing of your own standpoint means that your standpoint is everywhere. As self you are everywhere. That's the meaning of the text in the Kena Upanishad and the Ishā Upanishad: you see yourself in all living beings, the self-being of all. What does that mean?

Everything and everyone in the world has their own standpoint, that is a self-being. Now, these standpoints are your own standpoints. You are everything, literally. You are yourself everywhere and you are nothing special in a limited sense.

Is the subject then without an object?

In the falling away of everything there is the Inexpressible. In experience, the inside-out being-experience of unity comes together with the experience of outside-in. In and out, subject and object, completely flow through one another. You can no longer separate them. That is non-duality.

Take a look at what it really means when your final standpoint dissolves. You, yourself, dissolve. It's no wonder then that fear often arises in the remaining 'I'-residue, a fear of losing all control. The control is not only over actions, but also over perceptions. In the perception of the world there is already a strong application of force. Through perception everything receives a certain form and place and is immediately labeled: "this is this" and "that is that", everything in order. Everything that is seen is classified in a certain way according to a particular standpoint. There is a use of force there, a touch of violence. You fashion the world for yourself: this is reality and not otherwise.

But sometimes the entire reality corresponding to that perspective shifts and the categorization falters. Your standpoint and perspective don't appear to be so very stable. Now and then you see that your viewpoint changes. It can also entirely dissolve.

You see the struggle between standpoints in society. Everyone calls out, "Come here, come here, come here; this is a good perspective." Whichever perspective you take, you immediately have a certain definition of reality and so of yourself. Now the advaita teacher also says: "Come here, to the edge of the cosmos and see what I see." That is dangerous, because if you really go with it, it means the end of yourself as a standpoint. There is a reversal of every perspective, an eruption, into countless viewpoints, the inside-out. That is liberation, namely from every standpoint.

So actually it is very simple. When you just let it happen.

So liberation is actually unconditional love.

Yes of course, because it is a complete emotional acceptance of everything and everyone as yourself, the acceptance of the self of the other as yourself, also the emotional falling away of every separation. That indeed is love. You are everything and everyone. That is the real meaning of "love your neighbor as yourself". The quality of consciousness comes with this love because you are universal being-awareness and love-being without a center.

5.7 Joy

Hoorneboeg, October 17, 2004

Hopefully it is clear now to everyone. Joy arises by itself when more space comes, when there is an expansion of your own experienced being-space. Expansion of your self-being is instantaneous joy. You sit down, it's quiet, you relax and there is expansion. The borders fall away and immediately there is joy. This joy develops directly. Yesterday we discussed the development of joy, moving from the cruder emotional energies on the physical level, through more psychological feelings towards a further development which includes cosmic bliss, ānanda, without forms, without boundaries. Joy, love, happiness have the tendency to expand outwards from a limited state. They have an impulse within themselves, a certain movement in the direction of the infinite. When you don't block this movement, there is truly divine joy beyond all forms and conditions. You are that joy.

It always comes back to being aware of your own situation. We speak about recognizing all the different possibilities, so that you know where you are at a particular time period and how it can continue to develop. On every level, anytime, anywhere, it is the same: can there be a little more space? Yes? Excellent. Then once again you experience a further expansion and so also once again the springing up of joy. In the infinite sphere of sat-chit-ananda there is a very fine undifferentiated quality of joy, happiness, love. It is said that creation, thus the development in a coarser direction, arises in order to receive this kind of experience in a stronger and more aware manner. Just be aware of all levels. When the sphere is very refined, the joy is very subtle. Then there is no person who enjoys it. You are formlessly present internally in the sphere, yet with an inner knowledge of it. When this expresses itself on coarser levels up to the physical, the experience can be very strong, for example: the heart meditation.

Experience that joy has nothing to do with thinking. With joy you aren't sitting in your head thinking. When you resume thinking, the laughing quickly disintegrates because thinking can so easily close you off. The recognition of the sphere of joy allows you to realize: wonderful, my own sphere of energies, which can develop by itself and in which I am myself. That is expansion, that is joy. Thought easily recreates boundaries, certain categories in which everything becomes contained. When an emotion becomes so strong that it crosses over the border, then the 'I'-think has a tendency to try to restore order.

It's clear that true feelings and emotions are not restricted by the boundaries of thought. They can't be caught and held in a concept. In psychology you can certainly categorize emotions, but you cannot contain them. The emotional sphere precedes thought and goes beyond it. Mood and emotion are already present before an 'I'-thought is formed. If you remain only on the level of "I do", "I want", "I think" then you are a pawn of your pre-existing emotions and impulses. The ego serves those impulses. Therefore it's good to get to know these realms in a conscious way. You can literally go from head to heart. Then you notice that it is a more original sphere. You feel that everything is more fluid. The emotional energies come in waves. They cannot be contained by thought. They flood the 'I'-think. They easily develop cosmic dimensions. Then there is no more 'I'.

So you see the relativity of the 'I'-world, even with respect to the emotional sphere. You see how relative the world of the 'I'-think is. So don't make it more important that it is. In clarity everything becomes obvious. You see the relativity of the limited 'I'-sphere and the misery it creates when you enclose yourself there. Become aware once again of the greater space and joy.

In clarity it also becomes clear how relative your emotions are. They are your local energy clouds with a particular quality. From the greater spaciousness you see their relativity. In the presence of the greater space, these more concentrated emotional energies continue to develop. They absorb space whenever they can. And so in this way they dissolve. In the sky above the heath you can see the clouds slowly dissolve into the blue. This illustrates the general law of nature called entropy, which states that a concentrated energy becomes universally and homogeneously distributed precisely as it receives more space. This natural order also applies to emotional energies. Just give these energies more space in your being-awareness. Then they resolve. In that dissolution joy develops. The latter is the universal being-awareness-joy. True joy, real happiness knows no form, but is universal. [...]

You have always known this joy. You recognize it from before, long before. Everyone comes from a sphere where it was present. The first step of the creation takes place in the sphere of positive joy, although it is still quite rarified. It is the positivity of expansion in the form of creation that is positive and joyful. If a negative quality should exist there, everything would immediately become cramped and halted. Then the creation would not be able to continue. God joyfully creates the creation, because he/she finds it wonderful. "And God said it was good." This original joy precedes the ups and downs of the world. So whatever kind of traumas exist in the world, they are always secondary with respect to the original joy and divinity. Thus the point is to recognize something of that joy even in the trauma and brokenness. Then the foundation is good and all traumas dissolve within it. It is the space that is greater than everything. So everything dissolves within it.

Whether it's about simpler problems now, or more serious ones such as in psychiatry, or the essential problems such as those encountered within the advaita approach, it's always about the same thing: experience the spaciousness that was there before the problem appeared. The space always remains. You are that space. Then immediately there is again joy and that joy becomes a motor for continued expansion and dissolution. This joy, this pleasure, has the tendency to become infinite.

Perhaps you remember it well from long ago. Also, you see it again in young children. Whenever they take pleasure in something, for example in running fast or going crazy, the joy and the enthusiasm keeps increasing. So they keep going and the process keeps going indefinitely, if it doesn't meet with resistance. Of course, sometimes there is a collision between the momentum and the hard world and then the enthusiasm ends in tears. Still, the principle of the infinite joy is certainly there. If just a little tiny spark gets its chance, 'fft!' and again it's infinite.

Douwe, isn't it a pity that all this gets forgotten when you grow up? Then the 'I'-consciousness comes with its limited thinking and then you have to find it all over again.

You can't remain a child. There is growth, the world is hard, others don't accept it. The confrontation with hard materiality and the social world takes care of the process with which an 'I' is formed. Then there is separation. However, longing for the return or expansion into infinity remains. The knowledge of it remains. That's the basis of longing.

Then what's the real difference between such a child and the enlightened state?

It's the being-awareness, the conscious recognition. When you clearly see the process of separation, you understand the everyday, dual situation. Then you also see that which precedes it, that which is much more essential and which is always already there. This original self does not need to be connected to the physical body. Only when you identify yourself with the physical body do you become conditioned by the materiality because then there is a collision between the self and the world. So, go back to your original identity and see that it is just as it was before: the non-dual, original sphere. It is right there and it is your own true being. The ignorance of the child in paradise becomes a knowing-being, so that now there is no cycle, no *samsāra,* nothing additional is needed to know That.

Light meditation

Look towards the blue sky that is filled with sunlight and with closed eyes direct yourself towards the sun. If there is no blue sky and sun to see, close your eyes and imagine that you see the sky and the sun before you. Experience the infinity of the heavens and also the radiation of the sun with awareness.

a) Become aware of the feeling in the region of your heart and let your heart open. This is possible when you feel the space before and above you. Then let the sunlight radiate into your heart. More light increasingly enters your heart, until you radiate just like the sun in the entire space.
b) Imagine that you fly upwards, ever more into the radiating space, into the radiating light. Just experience that you enter increasingly into the heavenly sphere of light, increasingly taking on the quality of light and coinciding with it.

How big are you now?

Are there borders and separations still present?

As light, do you change?

Do you also see the worldly manifestations of light as manifestations of your own light?

Can you experience that your quality of universal light becomes more refined and has the tendency to dissolve into the inexpressible?

5.8 Ānanda, peace

Schiermonnikoog, June 9, 2001

[...] You are often talking about your own unhappy little 'I'. But you also spoke about your experience "when I walk with awareness of the outer and inner world, there is no 'I' that walks; there is space and that is also consciousness."

Yes.

Then you don't need to say "but". You confirm genuine openness for yourself.

Yes, but where is ānanda then, the bliss? Or does it mean that it's empty...

Don't create an image of it. Instead take a closer look: there is only space and somewhere walking continues, but you don't specifically identify yourself with that walking. You confirm the sphere of self-being, about which nothing can be said, which has no localization. Return there again very precisely. So, move to nowhere.

Yes.

From here to nowhere. You confirm: you are the empty consciousness-sphere. You are everywhere and nowhere. You have nothing, you own nothing, but you are everything. Everything is present in your own sphere. It's a wonderful sphere.

But when I walk along the beach, I see only the beach. No solar systems or anything.

"When I walk along the beach..."; but you didn't walk, there was no looking with eyes, nor a projection of expectations about solar systems. There was walking and there was an experience-sphere about which you have nothing to say, except that there were no boundaries. Stay with that.

I do that when I walk.

If that is the case, then you don't have to do anything special anymore with walking; you don't have to do anything special anymore that is specific to seeing. It happens by itself, but your being-sphere is that of infinite being-awareness. When that is truly present, when that clearly manifests itself...

Yes.

Isn't that *ānanda*?

For me these are glimpses, I think.

Stop thinking. Stay with the sphere that is there. Confirm that there are no boundaries, you are not situated in the walking, you are not situated in the seeing and there is an infinite being-sphere. You look around you and you turn around… and everything is loose and free. Everything is good just as it is.

It's neither good nor bad.

In any case, there is nothing that you need to resist, including painful experiences and difficult circumstances. In that sense everything is allowed to be. When the good and not-good are allowed to exist, then you have a kind of Goodness which goes beyond the oppositions of the daily goodness and not-goodness. Everything is allowed to exist just as it is without judgment. In that sense, it is good.

This also has to do with *ānanda*. When you, on the personal 'I'-level, create certain ideas about enlightenment, when you imagine that enlightenment must be an amazingly beautiful and great experience, then enlightenment stands in opposition to difficult experiences.

It is grand…

When there really is a breakthrough, it means a breaking through of all categories of thought, including the little compartments of beautiful experiences and not-beautiful experiences. Just as the goodness remains, in the sense that everything is allowed to be, you also have a happiness that remains. After the breakthrough something remains that is independent of the categories of thought, that is beyond them. If we have used words for it that are borrowed from the personal world, you must realize that the content no longer belongs to the personal world, but is a universal last quality. So also, *ānanda* is not an idea from a person who says that there should be beautiful experiences. That has nothing to do with it, because, by contrast, later he will be very unhappy, for example when the sun becomes hidden by the clouds.

Go back to your experience-sphere of walking. You can't say anything about it, but at least there is something that, in a very fine and universal way, has to do with the feeling: yes, it is good, positive, it is happiness, bliss. These words are borrowed from the idea of the bliss of the 'I', but what they refer to is something entirely different. Here it's about the last echo, on the level of the most subtle and universal energy. Thus, bliss is very refined and open, no longer concentrated somewhere with the heat and weight of personal emotionality. On this last level, it is within time. Yet the great bliss is something that remains. You might find that it is bare and empty. Many people buy a return ticket and go back again. They find their personal situation is not always pleasant, but at least it's a lot more fun. That's great, but then suddenly they get stuck again. Once more, there is suffering, because they want to hold on to that cozy sphere.

I can certainly imagine that there is satisfaction, that there are no conflicts.

Yes, Peace, with a capital 'P', is also a beautiful word. There is infinite Peace.

happiness
just happiness
in happiness there is only happiness
plop and it's there
immediate, original
grace
without anyone receiving that grace, because
in happiness there is only happiness
just happiness
happiness

5.9 Bhakti

Gouda, December 5, 1998

During one period of time there were evenings in which the emphasis was on loving devotion (*bhakti*), because it was useful for opening up on the emotional level. It was useful because we looked at the nature of feeling more precisely. Let's continue with that now.

Go back to your own concrete, physical situation. Usually your own physical sphere is not homogeneous. There are harder and softer areas. Now we can look more precisely at the latter. It is a study of yourself, now on the level of the emotions. In any case this is to be found very near the heart region. Pay more attention to the source of feelings. Through this they can be released.

Take note of the location from which you look out at everything, the position of your own 'I' as perceiver. Usually the location is rather high, in the head. Let yourself descend from there, let yourself sink further down in the direction of your heart region. Take note of the physical sphere in which you are now present: what about its softness and hardness? There are hard and soft structures. You can palpably establish where it's harder and where it's softer. You can probably experience that it is soft somewhere in the heart region. You can see that for yourself. You can go there more and more. You can approach it palpably. You feel how it is, very concretely! Once you find the location of the tender heart-feeling, it becomes stronger as you go there more often. In contrast to the harder areas, the core of the heart is soft and fluid and the fluidity increases because you give it attention. Then the feeling energy also flows. It is a very dynamic feeling. It is a wave, continuously moving to and fro. The wave motion increases in strength. Just experience it as a strong wavelike energy, initially as liquid. It is a fluid light energy. Inhale and the energy goes within, exhale and the energy flows outwards, radiating in all directions. It's a very clear feeling, but perhaps you can also view it as luminous energy. Otherwise, visualize it so that you can experience it for yourself very concretely. When you see it very clearly before you, you can go into it slowly, so that internally you flow along with the dynamic movement, with the waves and the radiations. Let yourself sink more deeply into it. From the head with its consciousness let yourself continuously sink down into the emotions, into the heart. In this way head and heart, consciousness and emotion come together.

Consciously return once again to your starting location in your head and then look towards the heart feeling. You confirm what there is to confirm. You do that from a mental standpoint or in any case from a position of consciousness. You as consciousness are more than just a mental clarity, more than a theoretical clarity. You are a being-awareness, an aware presence being, one aspect of which is feeling. In your own aware sphere there is a distinct feeling energy present, a feeling energy in which you are involved. That feeling element should become integrated, so that it doesn't remain an object, as it does in psychology. When you remain situated at the level of consciousness, you keep yourself distant from your feeling and so you retain an internal split. When you, as being-awareness, descend into the feeling region, the duality disappears and the feeling sphere becomes lucid from the inside-out.

Frequently the heart energy has a quality of longing. That longing arises because there is a separation between yourself as desire energy and the desired. Mental thoughts play a large role in this separation. Your emotional energy is kept within certain limits. The 'I'-think continually says: you are physically present here with this form and this feeling; over there are other things from which you are separated, but they really belong to you.

When you let yourself descend into the sphere of the heart energy, is there still that separation, is there still that desire? When as thinker you completely sink into the heart energy, you experience that all separation disappears. When the 'I'-think ends up in the emotional sphere, the structures of the ego tend to disappear. The ego is nothing more than a hard structure, a hard energetic structure which can become fluid once again. It becomes fluid when you realign yourself with the streaming heart energy. Everything dissolves there, including the edges that the energy initially had. You surrender and then notice how the energy directly and automatically develops cosmic dimensions.

Be careful of the transition in the internal movement towards the heart. When you retreat a little into your head, you have separation again with limitations and longing. When you truly let yourself sink into the heart energy, all limitations disappear. Let the heart energy ignite, until it becomes a great fire in which your 'I', yourself, dissolves. Perhaps initially you experience that the heart energy is like a small candle flame, but later the flame becomes a great bonfire which consumes everything that is rigid. It also strikes out. It also consumes physical boundaries.

Internally in the feeling sphere you are present as being-awareness, without borders, infinite. There is one great ocean of feeling being-awareness. Be careful as soon as forms and boundaries return. Notice that it is an activity of your thought. Then it's important to fully return once again to the realm of the heart energy. Then the separations disappear once again and also there is no more longing, because everything that was desired has been assimilated into the whole. There is a deep and universal bliss. Sat (being), cit (consciousness), and ānanda (bliss) come together. That is the core of all mysticism. At first a separation is experienced that is very painful and which people want to transcend. Then there is a movement towards the core of your heart. You don't need to lug an entire theology in there. You can call the core of your heart divine, but then it appears to be the infinite sphere of your Self and, simultaneously, of everything. Thus, the realization of unity is not difficult, it is very near, so close that you overlook it. But by staying alert and returning to the core of your feeling-Self, you experience how it is: you are infinite love.

You know what must happen. So then you can just let it happen.

Everything comes in Love.
Everything goes in Love.
Everything comes and goes in the infinite Love
of being-everything-Self-awareness.

5.10 Light

Hoorneboeg, October 9, 2005

Do you experience the great light outside? And do you experience the light from within, from your own consciousness and your heart? Go further within, further within, further within.

The light of consciousness coincides with the light of the heart. As you withdraw further you see that the internal light and the external light are coming towards each other and will coincide. When you can really experience that, then you also experience that it is a type of nuclear fusion. The light becomes extremely intense with a wonderfully strong energy. White light, the light of lightning, the white light of nuclear fusion.

What does that do? Do you experience it so that everything explodes? That white light of a thousand suns. Do you experience that not a single particle of 'I' remains? That you are absorbed into the light. Everything that does not have the same quality as that light evaporates in the heat; it disappears. So the self-being also evaporates in that greatness.

You are that original light, that initial energy from the big bang. From it everything emerges, into it everything returns. What remains? Perhaps a cosmos in which things clump together now and again; images that occasionally compose themselves a little and then disintegrate. The original light remains present in the foreground and you remain as that. All penetrating. Whatever else arises comes forth out of that original light. And through that light it is destroyed once again.

That all-consuming, intensely illuminating fire, you are that. Initially you may still have the sense that you have entered into that fire. Your last forms dissolve within it. Then everything is blank yet nevertheless there is an internal knowledge of it. You are internally present in that light, just as in dreamless sleep. Internally you are that bright sphere of dreamless sleep. Is that clear? Infinity of empty light, you are that, nothing else. Let this dimension stay open. Let it remain present. Even when the forms reappear.

Everything is dissolved in light. That's the function of light as fire. In fire everything is purified. Everything that is not pure is burned. Yesterday we talked about purgatory. It has something to do with that. Purgatory was not introduced merely as a concept. No, light has something to do with purification. As the light becomes stronger, as you come closer to it, everything that is dark enters into the light; simultaneously you experience an additionally purifying effect. Wonderful. But, the harder you hold on to your darker forms, the more problematic your situation becomes. When you hold on to it fully and firmly, it becomes a hell in which you are roasted.

So, just let everything go. Then see what happens. The light becomes your own sphere and your own light sphere is universal without separations. Light is everywhere and you are that light. Everything radiates light out of itself, from yourself. All is light.

Everything is light,
light that knows no boundary;
therefore there is no shadow,
no trace in the transparency;
the color play
of this infinite light
you are, I am,
as long as anything is;
everything is light.

5.11 The dreamless state

Gouda, June 13, 2005

During the day it works pretty well for me to stay alert in clarity, but in the evenings I become quite tired and fall asleep. I fall into a black hole and I think that's too bad. But, you do have to sleep in order to become fully rested.

To the extent that there is a busy life, you have to deal with a body, with its brain, mind and so on. Hence certain laws apply, such as the necessary alternations of activity and passivity, of waking and sleeping. Only, slowly something else emerges which goes beyond, a new kind of clarity. It's different from the consciousness of images, sounds, drowsiness, alertness and so forth. No, a very different clarity develops that is quite subtle. It's so subtle, that it's a confirmation of the blank state which is also present in dreamless sleep.

At night the unconscious goes on a mad rampage. Then everything is included, even unpleasant things.

In the dream state all kinds of different forms can arise that still have some energy in them. They will slowly fade away.

Yes, but there is still quite a lot.

Yes, then for the time being you have to accept it as it is.

Oh, so that's not so bad?

What is bad? Confirm for yourself that the most important thing is to remain aware in the blank state.

Yes, but that doesn't happen in sleep.

You just told me that you were aware in a sort of sleep state. If you stay open to it, a continuity of that very subtle consciousness increasingly develops. You experience and confirm that this aware blank state continues. At a certain point it continues on in sleep.

But I find it ridiculous that there are still so many things coming up in it. I'd really rather see the void.

Yes, but don't focus on it too much. The open sphere is so

subtle, it is nothing. So it's not a confirmation of anything. Return to yourself – the open sphere – to the extent that you have experienced and do experience it. Then it's a different sort of confirmation.

Different than in the waking state.

Waking consciousness is directed towards the world of forms, the world that you experience with your senses. But there is another consciousness that is aware of something that is much finer, much subtler than forms. It is always present, because it is free from the limitations of space and time.

But then will I still know it?

There is in you, here and now, a certain knowledge of that original source.

I don't believe it, or else I've got a wrong picture of it.

That's the point: you want to make an image of it, while that's not possible. It's a being-experience without any image. It's knowledge of nothing. If you still hold on to the old idea of knowledge, you say: "That doesn't exist." No, not like things exist. That's how it is for most people. If there's a blackout during the day, or a dreamless sleep at night, you don't remember anything of it when you return to the normal waking world.

No, but you said that you certainly can remember it.

When you return to the personal waking world, you don't remember anything, because you think that you have to remember something. Then you don't remember anything. The knowledge comes when you have recognized yourself as the blank state of dreamless sleep. That is easiest in a meditative sphere.

So OK, I can certainly see that. But that's not sleep.

Then you also see that it won't be ruptured by a dream state sleep, because you always already are that state of emptiness. Everyone is continually that infinite dreamless being. That is the most authentic self-being. In the formation of the 'I'-person a superstructure is built over it. Then there is an 'I'. You look outwards and have no idea where that looking originates from. Return to your Self.

Still, isn't it ruled out that you can't have consciousness while you are in a dreamless sleep, for the simple reason that afterwards you only know that you had a dreamless sleep? Or did I misunderstand?

That's right. When you wake up as an 'I'-person you say: "I slept really well, but I can't remember anything; so it was a dreamless sleep." But, in your case, that's a conclusion drawn in hindsight. Here we're talking about an ongoing confirmation: "This is my own, never absent self-sphere."

So, in other words, the three states of waking, dreaming and dreamless sleep play out in your own self-sphere.

When you stay aware in your own original self-sphere, then that's obvious. But be careful that it's not a post facto confirmation or a conclusion. See that it remains the greatest ongoing reality.

So, from the moment that you enter into the dreamless sleep, you know that you are in the dreamless sleep.

Yes, but don't make any conceptual representation out of it. Take a look at your own experience where something of it is recognized, for example in deep meditation. You can recognize something of it there. Then you also notice that the 'state' is independent of time and space. When you dive back into the body from a deep meditative state and you notice the clock, you see that somehow a long period of time has passed. So time has nothing to do with that 'state'. Nevertheless you have a knowledge of it. Perhaps it is quite strange: that you can have knowledge of a sphere of your own that is not in time or space.

I enter into very refined regions,
into cosmic spaces, far, very far.

When a reminder of my body pops up,
there is loneliness and fear.

But the light and the space let me
leave everything behind.

I even lose all form and
come free
into nothing,
the open self of everything.

That's how death will be.
That's how life with death is.

5.12 The non-duality of groundless openness inside and out

Bruges, November 7, 2004, notes from a talk taken by an attendee

In deep relaxation and silence all phenomena come and go. Only the Original remains. This Great overtakes the world of the 'I'. Be aware of that. The Great is not apart from you: it is your own self. It is that encompassing dimension which includes everything in itself. In the return to yourself you forget yourself and merge into that Great.

To the extent that you don't completely forget yourself, the Great will wipe away the rest of you and that is the experience of dying. Here, too, the readiness for surrender is necessary: "not my will, but thy will be done".

Return to the origin of self-being. You will confirm that there never was a separation between yourself and the absolute. Recognize that very clearly. You are sitting; everything relaxes; you completely open up. When you release your whole identity, you coincide with the Great. Then there are no borders any longer. In the open sphere, everything is allowed to be.

With meditation you let the attention that is usually directed outwards to the world turn back to yourself. Your attention expands inwardly and becomes open. The focal point of attention can then coincide with the source of yourself. Then there is no duality any longer; there is no separation any longer between yourself and the observed. Subject and object come together. There is no observer and no observed. There is only an infinite being-awareness.

When you are aware of that great silent sphere, then all elements of physicality disappear. All 'I' notions cease to exist. This depth of silence is always already present. During your meditation you recognize it. It is so obvious.

On the level of the witness-consciousness there is still a physicality. When it goes well, the bodily localization of the witness dissolves in a very deep relaxation. In the relaxation every distance disappears. There is the universal heavenly unity of 'I am'. That also dissolves in the final relaxation. It is surrender unto the Great. The 'I' has already been purified. The final qualities of yourself disappear. Only the great silence still remains. You are that deep silence. All separations have fallen away, including with the Great. You come home to what was Nothing. Nothing more is necessary. In the inexpressible openness there is nothing more to say.

Letting everything open *there*
the self-being opens here:
one openness.

5.13 Self-being and non-duality with the external openness

With the inquiry into self-being there turn out to be various levels of self-being on the 'vertical' axis of consciousness: ego, witness, universal self and the absolute. At each level there is a particular kind of non-duality.

Ego

People experience many separations. That sense of separation is especially strong between "my own" (I, we) and what is foreign (the other, the strange). Nevertheless there are all kinds of situations in which that duality does not exist or at least is less evident. Non-duality is present, for example, during sleep, in silent, thought-free moments during the day, in enjoyment and in being happy. Then there is a deeper layer of existence with less separateness which rises to the surface, or a higher dimension opens – use whatever metaphor you wish – so that this can be consciously experienced. This lack of separation is continually buried below the daily sphere of consciousness by the 'I'-in-the-world (ego) or in the psychological notion of a good feeling or experience. Then, for example, it is said: "I had such a beautiful experience of unity… " Then non-duality is just something that arises sometimes as an experience of an 'I' without actually affecting that 'I'.

Witness

The recognition of non-duality can develop by taking on a detached point of view in consciousness. Entanglement in the dualistic world then loses its strength. Everything is observed from the higher viewpoint of the 'witness', including your own functioning in the world, your whole little life. Everything is reflected as if it is in a mirror. In the witness as reflexive consciousness you have partially separated from your identity as a person in the world and all kinds of conditionings that influence your perception of the world have disappeared. The physical heaviness and your interconnectedness to it have, to a large extent, dissolved. You have become freer. You're really nothing more than consciousness with a consciousness-space in which everything appears. There is non-duality here in so far as the phenomena appear within your own consciousness-space. Everything is located within your own perceiving-being.

Nevertheless, the structure of separation still remains through this inner withdrawal into the consciousness-space, the distance between yourself, as perceiver, and existence, as the perceived. That remains so, even as the process of taking distance and the reflexive experience, now of the perceiver, is repeated.

This basic structure with a separated first and third person will disappear when the power of the 'I' to maintain its existence and defend its world disappears. This is possible because there is something greater, a larger space than the witness-consciousness.

The universal self

Sooner or later in spiritual development the experience of the great external openness and the surrender to it takes place. Sometimes it occurs early due to a great sensitivity for it, sometimes later, only after a long period of internal withdrawal, purification and deepening of understanding, when most of the limitations of the ego have been released. It's about letting go of the last standpoint and perspective, of releasing the last knot. This happens automatically when the 'I' as perceiver of phenomena is released. By making a quarter-turn rotation of yourself inwardly as perceiver you can further expand your attention for phenomena and experience the greater space more consciously. This can also help to shift the focus of attention towards the space itself.

When the final standpoint of the witness has disappeared, you are an infinite self-sphere without a center. It is one whole, without duality. Within that everything happens by itself in an inclusive way. In that one great ocean you no longer have form and location, but the universal qualities are still present: feeling-being, consciousness, bliss-being. There is softness, fluidity, refinement. You coincide with the infinity of the blue sky, the divine light. Then there is an end to the deficiency that was present in duality, to the longing to fill that lack and the suffering caused by the impossibility of ever doing so. Here, everything is absorbed in your own cosmic consciousness.

Everyone always already has a sense of this realm of consciousness, bliss-being, free-being. Everyone always already is this infinity.

The absolute

The great external openness appears to have an even further reaching aspect than cosmic greatness, namely absolute groundlessness without qualities. This indicates that the universal divine sphere is also relative, that is, it is connected to an 'I' and still as space in time. That 'I' is the self of the being ('I am') and of the being of the qualities ("I am being, consciousness, bliss"). A radical liberation means that even this 'I am' is also released.

When the existence of that 'I' is no longer defended, 'I am' and the great qualities appear to become finer until the 'I'-self with the last qualities merges into that about which nothing more can be said: the absolute. 'I', as subject of perception and actions, as first person, appears to have an infinite depth. The depth of self-being ultimately appears to be the groundless openness which coincides with that of the world-ground. As absolute, there is the non-duality of the highest being and the highest self-being without qualities, of the absolute on the subject and object side. The being of the world and the self-being are merged therein. Still there is an irreducible sense of it and this is possible because your deepest self-being is one with That.

When there is a creation, when a world pops up, it comes from the absolute openness. Without foundation it is the foundation of everything. From the undifferentiated, comes the first differentiation between being and self-being (consciousness). Afterwards the many mental, physical and world forms emerge. The original openness is thus the condition required for the possibility of the world; the openness of self-being then is the condition for the possibility of knowledge of the world. Chapter 6 is about the relationship between the absolute and the world. This also appears to be a non-duality.

All separations have disappeared;
I am the self of everything and
also, I am everything:
where is the longing, what is there still to fear?

And yet the other is still there;
even though I am the other and
of that other, I am the self,
because all separations have disappeared.

6

The non-duality of the absolute and the relative

There is non-duality not only between the open essences of being and self-being, which was treated in the previous chapter, but there is also a non-duality between this openness and the world of forms in space and time. The restricted and the unrestricted, form and emptiness, coincide without problems because the absolute itself is unconditioned. Life and the world continue on in that openness. They remain transparent before the infinite depth, which is also the depth of self-being. The non-duality of the absolute and the relative is an indescribable groundless openness; though also, an openness which reveals itself very simply in everyday life.

With the raising of my gaze there is infinite space,
in listening, the infinite harmony of sounds.
I smell the infinitely fine fragrance
and taste the immortal nectar.
With my hands I touch the infinitude,
as body I am all that, in infinite expansion.
As infinite consciousness I see the universal finitude.
I am
all that
as nothing.

6.1 Everything goes on in the openness

Sometimes there is something, sometimes nothing – from a letter exchange, August, 2008

You often say: "Sometimes there is something, sometimes nothing… " or "As long as there is life… " These statements come from a certain position, a certain perspective. What perspective is that, exactly?

When you begin to speak about perspectives, there are an infinite number of them. No particular position is permanent or more important than any other. They always exist in connection to realities, each of which is determined by the possibilities and conditions of the corresponding viewpoint. No particular reality is permanent or more important than any other reality.

Self-being is absorbed-being in that inexpressible from which the standpoints and worlds arise and in which they have a place. The infinite number of standpoints are the immanent aspect of the indescribable being-self-being (Âtman-Brahman). It is present everywhere, though it remains transcendent, free of the cosmos. "Sometimes there is something, sometimes nothing" refers to that inexpressible.

When, in that inexpressible, there is a body as viewpoint, it means that in its terms (senses, nervous system, etc.) there is a special world. "So long as there is life" refers to this body and world.

Free-being remains, although everything continues normally – from a letter exchange, February, 2002

I listened several times recently to a recording from an advaita teacher which made me uncomfortable. He said that we are Consciousness. He said that if you see THAT once, you won't cry any longer when someone dies. He told an anecdote about two jnanis (enlightened masters) attending a funeral who went to the bathroom to moisten their eyes in order to appear grief stricken, but didn't feel any sorrow. Great, that might be so for them, but I am form, too. Then can't I also affirm that this form feels grief when someone dies or laughs when this form is happy? How can you not feel the emotions that rightly belong to such a form?

There is a frequent misunderstanding on this point. Advaita is the unproblematic coinciding of formless being-awareness and form. As long as there is form, there are the processes and experiences that belong to such a form. To the extent that an individual is "realized in this lifetime", there are the normal things that belong to being human. Only: then, these are not different from the formless Inexpressible. They no longer possess the restricting power that they normally have in human existence. Free-being remains, even though everything continues normally. Nisargadatta Maharaj cried with real tears when his wife died. There are jnana-yogis who have withdrawn themselves into emptiness through renunciation of their emotional life. They have closed off their being and feeling-being. Because this is one-sided and dualistic, they haven't fully realized the non-duality.

Can I come back to my question again? By chance I listened today to a tape of another advaita teacher, who said in a similar vein: Either you see the little head or you see Consciousness.

Don't hold onto statements spoken in a particular context. When you return to the source of your Self – that is literally always going further, further back and completely surrendering there – everything appears to have the quality of consciousness. The forms remain, as long as they are there, but don't appear to be any different than consciousness. The 'either… or' disappears into the one, endless non-duality.

Becoming like a child – Gouda, 2002

We have spoken now and then about "becoming like a child". The child is still present in everyone. When you go back deeply enough you can always rediscover the child within, the child who was totally open and felt an inner connectedness with everything and everyone. This creates the recognition that that is your natural way of being: being without borders.

Through the rediscovery and recognition of your natural being, your situation rises above that of a child. Namely, now there is an awareness of it. The child does not have that and so is easily indoctrinated into the idea of being a person. Therefore it is easily captivated by phenomena. Since you now experience the open self-sphere in a conscious way, no one can delude you anymore. So you don't deceive yourself either.

Outpouring love – Schiermonnikoog, June 16, 2006

Let's look again at the important process of releasing yourself by allowing yourself to flow outwards into the world. That's how it was at the top of the sand dune here. It is a literal outwards flow and expansion of your energetic body with which you are usually identified. As that process continues, a cosmic body arises. You are everything.

Your energetic body is a feeling body. When you experience this very clearly, you leave the level of solid matter in which you were initially present. The emotional energy is fluid and can easily flow outwards. As it flows, you release the old form and it dissolves. Because you were identified with the bodily form, you release yourself from the limited form. The release of the form means the release of the egocentricity, because you flow outwards in all directions. The cramped center dissolves. In your experience you become free of the form and become a universal being, very sensitive, touching and feeling. It is truly a loving outpouring of one's self-being, so that there is no opposition between the one and the other, between the 'I' and the other. It is the acceptance of the other as yourself, literally. That is love. In love, everything is included as your own.

So you can imagine yourself once again up there on the dune. Slowly, everything becomes fluid in your own bodily sphere and flows down the slope. It's like an amoeba with its plasma flowing outwards. It is not an imperialistic capture and control of whatever exists in the environment. No, it's a release of yourself and thus becoming one.

It is an outflow of yourself in love towards the other. Do you then see that the quality of the other also changes? When you truly let your own energy as love-energy go out towards the other, you come together there with the other in love. Also, when you take a little distance, you see that there is another quality in the other. Which quality? You will be very tempted to say: I love the other person. Why? You have loved the other as yourself, because, literally, your self is present in the other.

As that flow goes outwards in all directions, towards everything and everyone, you experience yourself as the self of all. 'You' and 'the self of all' are ultimately no longer demonstrable things, but instead groundless openness. Within it everything continues normally.

Is that clear? Does that correspond with your own experience?

Hearing the mountain stream is
becoming the mountain stream, because
the babbling finds
no resistance in me:
swirling and sparkling, I flow
downstream.

6.2 The inside-out

Gouda, January 17, 2007

As you turn further and further within, there can still be an 'I'-consciousness for a long time. As the relaxation in your own depth continues and as you remain lucid, that 'I'-consciousness becomes freed and becomes universal. First there is a consciousness of the outside world. Self, as 'I'-consciousness, is positioned somewhere in the body, within, and the rest is outside.

As you go further within with an ever deepening relaxation, the 'I'-consciousness relaxes and completely opens, infinitely. Thus what was external comes together with what was internal. On the one hand the outside comes in, the world into the consciousness-sphere. On the other hand, through your opening inside-out, your self-being is present everywhere in the cosmos.

Is that clear? Can that also happen in your own experience? As your point of attention on external things returns sufficiently far within, further back than the viewpoint of the witness, to the core of yourself, everything seems to flip inside-out by itself. Your own innermost core – that you are – totally reverses and then is present everywhere, including everything that was initially external. That inner journey can take place in your consciousness, towards yourself as witness-consciousness, and then proceed even further into the core yourself. That can also happen in the direction of your heart.

This is indicated in many passages in the classical texts. It is repeatedly said in the Upanishads: Return to your heart; there is a small flame or a lotus; it is incredibly small; but if you go inside there, you notice that it contains everything. Pascal also said the same thing: man is an incredibly vulnerable speck in the universe. What is he on the scale of the cosmos? A fragile piece of reed. Nevertheless, as spirit, man contains everything: the inside is out. Both perspectives go together.

Everyone knows this reversal in their relationship with others. When you are objectified by someone – "You are an x…" – you have the tendency to survive the attack by turning within. Then the relationship structure easily flips: the internal becomes larger than the external. From out of your own greater space you relativize the other with his statements and attack. Even if you don't have a conflict with the other, nevertheless all externals are contained within yourself by turning within. When you release both points of view, every problem disappears. Everyone knows this. It's very simple.

Another illustration: a potter once succeeded in turning a teapot inside out. Take a look [it was displayed in a glass cabinet at the Advaita Center]. First there was tea inside, then the pot was turned inside out and zzzzzt the tea is everywhere. Then there is always enough tea.

You can extend this. When you desire something, your desires are situated in the object of your desire. Through the orientation of your longing, your attention is there, in that object which you desire. You are present there. Your inner transposes itself outwards into the desired. Then the inside is out. You go infinitely along with the immeasurable longing and everything reverses. The desired and yourself are universally present. Thus, all longings are fulfilled. The entire structure of orientation on something else has disappeared. There are no desires any more. See that quite clearly!

In all examples the separation disappears. The whole dualistic structure of inner and outer disappears.

At first you have an idea that you sit enclosed within the form of your body and that your body is in space. When you truly go within, this structure turns inside-out, literally! Your self-being appears to be outside as universal space. See the teapot with the inside out. The tea which was in the teapot is now outside. The tea is universal. So also, you appear to be universal.

You see your body, the earth, the universe reverse, shrink and fall into the great space of yourself. So also you are everything that still exists. Your own internal space, that self-being-awareness, becomes universal, literally. Then there is no more localization of yourself. Then too there isn't any concentrated attention on a particular object within that space. The being-awareness has become totally open. It has no center any more. There is no structure "I see this; I am aware of that" any longer. The beginning point and the end point, the conscious origin and the object as goal, no longer exist. They have come together and exploded into infinity. So it's not only about the relational structure turning around and then watching everything from the great consciousness, or establishing that everything is consciousness, but rather the inner has coincided with outer. Your own being-awareness has coincided with the great self-being in a non-duality.

But surely, isn't there still a form ready for action?

To the extent that forms are there, there are forms. You are the self of all these forms and you are much more.

Have you ransacked space looking for yourself?
And have you found anything yet?
You see:
How strange is the self.
It slips from your grasp, but
it's not anywhere.
It's present everywhere, but
the eye can't see it.
The empty self of all is wonderful,
the conflictless coinciding of
all and nothing.

6.3 Natives and foreigners

Gouda, January 8, 2005

When the news reports came about the tsunami disaster, I didn't have a personal reaction, though I did feel a connectedness.

There are all different kinds of possibilities. It's good when you can experience the disaster as an act of nature, without a sentimental reaction. Then there is a space in which the event takes place as something irreducible. A disaster like this happens - just like that. You can certainly say something about it, but actually, you can't say anything about it. Words simply fall short. Personal interpretations and emotional reactions are unequal to the magnitude of this event. But on the other hand, you are all that as well, including the suffering of the people living there. That's more than connectedness, more than the feeling of connectedness.

Yes, but I said to myself: if you were actually involved, you'd be singing a different song.

It depends on what the connectedness looks like. Even with a spiritual sensitivity you still experience that connectedness from a feeling of detached security. That's still possible from a supra-personal level, a level on which you continue to store personal elements. Then you have pity, or compassion on a level somewhat above that of the person. Pity and even compassion remain connected to a viewpoint through which something is experienced. I spoke about the falling away of every separation, every separation between yourself and the people there. You can recognize the non-duality directly. Then you also have the viewpoint of the people who are there on the spot. Then everything breaks open and there is more than connectedness. Then there is unity. When that happens, you fully accept the suffering and the deaths of the people there.

You become involved in the thought-world again so quickly. Then you no longer sit here on your chair, but go into your projections instead.

I wasn't talking about mental projections and entering into them, but about an openness in which everything that appears is also your own center.

I was living back in Iran and have now returned. I've picked up my life again here as if I'd never been away. This also happens when I go back to Iran.

So it seems that time isn't important for your own self-being, your own situation. In thought, time periods are positioned one after another, yet widely separated periods can also come together and even be present simultaneously. Then there aren't any chronological separations. To the extent that there is a spacious being-experience a spatial separation is also absent and isn't there between Iran and the Netherlands. There is only your universal identity which isn't dependent on time and space. You don't have to split up your identity into an Iranian and a Dutchman. Everything is simultaneously present here and now, you have an infinite number of individual identities, you are everywhere. All the possibilities can remain open, without zooming in on any particular spot. Whatever conditions and events exist on a practical level, it's all good. The one needn't stand in opposition to the other. All is one. You're at home everywhere.

When I'm here, I do miss my family, but not too much. I'm used to it by now.

What I meant was an even broader openness, in which both the one as well as the other can fully remain. Therefore, nothing happens. There are not different situations in which the one stands in opposition to the other. You are at home always and everywhere. You are free from conditions. That comes first. You are yourself everywhere. As self-being, we are all natives everywhere and foreigners in every particular situation. There needn't be psychological or social problems between these two.

It's not just in the Netherlands that I'm a foreigner, but also in Iran when I return there.

Yes, but you are also at home in all countries: native. Do you see that both coincide?

[Another visitor] I experience that I have different personalities. I'm different here than at my work and so on. I have a split-personality.

What I just said is that all the different identities can be present simultaneously. You have thousands of partial identities. These can remain open in the great whole of your Self-being. It's clear that there are different worldly situations and events. But openness means that all these possibilities remain open, free of time and space. The openness receives no specific interpretation, does not become fixed and therefore is also inexpressible.

So go into yourself, there, where you feel at home everywhere, while you also experience that you don't coincide with any particular situation, that you are as much native as foreigner.

That you are a foreigner everywhere means that you are free, that you are not stuck.

That you are native everywhere means that you are at home everywhere.

Why would you have a preference then for a particular situation?

When you are native everywhere, then why would you have a preference? Then it doesn't matter where you live.

It matters to me.

See to what extent it is important. When there is freedom, the practical situation is of relative importance. All events are irreducible. What happens, happens, including the tsunami. You have the sense that you have already lived thousands of lives, that you've already drowned in the waves many times. Now, one time more or less...

It has to do with the fundamental freedom, even though events continue to happen. You don't have to get stuck in them. Getting stuck happens when you can't accept situations. Then a specific identity remains, such as a Dutchman.

When I am in Iran, it's also good. There are only practical difficulties.

What is practical asks for practical action. Remain with the primary unlimited open self-being. The events, for example to go here or to go there, are the outcomes of practical forces and continue by themselves. Then there are no problems.

There is no self and even so I am everywhere
without a center and centered everywhere
I am the self of everything without self:
what a grief, what a joy.

6.4 Sensory non-duality

Gouda, May 14, 2008

Yes, we are always talking here about the recognition of non-duality. It's clear: in practice you should recognize very clearly that non-duality is the reality which dissolves duality and its associated suffering. You should determine this very clearly in your own experience.

It's easiest in the feeling sense. You can become aware of your tactile sensations. Imagine that the wind blows and that you experience the wind on your skin. Which reality is that? What do you really experience? There is a feeling in which you no longer experience the skin and the wind separately. In your experience it is one phenomenon. You can think further about it, that it has two sides, your skin and the wind, but what you experience is one phenomenon. You don't experience your skin and the wind separately. They have come totally together. It is *one* feeling phenomenon. Just call it skin-wind. Do you experience that skin-wind feeling in space? Do you see that your bodily self and what is said to come from outside are totally together? The wind, it blows. As skin-wind you go completely along with it into the infinite distance. You must forcibly intervene to pull the two apart from one another. In the feeling experience it's only about that one. That feeling, skin-wind. The wind is nothing without skin; the skin is nothing without wind. It is one phenomenon.

That's also true with the sense of taste, like when you eat an ice cream in this wonderful weather. How is it then? "Oh, what a delicious taste – strawberries, bananas… " What's that like? How is it with yourself in relation to the taste experience and that which you are tasting? Isn't that also only one? I recently read a Buddhist text on the idea of "one taste". The interpretation then was that you experience everything in the same way. There is no preference, and no denial. What is intended in the advaita approach is an even deeper meaning. In that one taste not only have the separations you make between the various experienced objects disappeared, but also between yourself, your experience, and the objects. Then there is not a separate "I taste" and "what I taste". Both have come together. There is one phenomenon of taste. Therefore the situation in which you clearly register that one taste or that one feeling has the tendency to become universal. Why? Because there are no divisions any longer. You taste something, a strawberry ice cream. As you enjoy the delicious taste, you easily enter into it. Then there is just "one taste" and that is universal. There is nothing else. You pick up the ice cream and there is still a distance; you bring it to your mouth, enjoy it and in the complete enjoyment there is a merging of yourself and the ice cream. You taste a strawberry ice cream and you're gone, the ice cream, too, is gone: one taste. What is the reality? You can't say anything more about it, except that you and the ice cream are one. So you clearly recognize non-duality on the sensory level: that's how it is.

In the hearing sense, separation also disappears. You hear beautiful music and you go right into it: the separation is gone. In going along with "I hear/am the music" it develops itself spatially and the literally-infinite enjoyment arises. [There is the sound of a fire engine in the distance.] You hear the sound of the siren and you cannot say whether it is somewhere outside, or whether it is present in your own sphere. There is a non-duality.

Seeing is highly dualistic, because seeing sets something up at a fixed distance. In the West everything exists at a distance because we are very visually oriented in our mentation. Duality reigns. But there is also another kind of seeing, a feeling-seeing, in which distance is not present. When you see from your heart, you notice that through your seeing you are in and with the things that you see. You see the light of the sun and you let the light enter into you. Every distance is gone. Sun and self are no longer separate. From out of your heart you see that self-light everywhere. You see someone else from your heart. The distance falls away and you can immediately determine: there is no duality with the other but rather a non-duality. You'd have to use force in order to maintain your distance towards the other. You'd have to make a real effort, paying attention to and maintaining that distance: "I am here and the other is there". When a little relaxation comes, you automatically sink in. You return to a sensitive seeing from your heart and the separation disappears. In relaxation it disappears automatically.

Keeping distance, that's tension. Look again at what happens when you keep that distance. Then there is a notion of yourself, regardless of what you see, regardless of the others that you see. The world, the others are kept at a distance. What appears there, what you see, is not allowed to come too close, not allowed into your territory. In that sense, you create a wall. In that sense you make yourself hard. In the energy of that distance-creating seeing is the energy that keeps the other at a distance. 'I' see 'you' there. Can you see the tension-keeping distance with each objectification? That also applies to all those different future events which people tend to fear: all those less attractive eventualities which must remain at a distance. Take a look on the energetic level. Then you immediately realize that the power which keeps everything at a distance, especially the things which are less pleasant, is contained within your seeing. So, relaxation means acceptance, such a complete acceptance that everything is allowed to come close, so close that it coincides with yourself. That applies also to the suffering that you see. Then there is more than just pity, more even than a compassion which still knows a distance. No, the other things and the other people are allowed to come so close that you coincide with them. That is the point of non-duality. There is no separation anymore between self-being and other-being.

Sensitive seeing from your heart, the feeling experience, is a very emotional being-awareness. Boundaries don't exist there. You can directly confirm: it is universal being-awareness.

Therefore there is also universal joy-being simultaneously. By allowing it to be open, there is universal aware-bliss-being. When you don't hold back and there is a deep relaxation, there is an immediate and very aware recognition of non-duality as the reality. So it's not just a feeling. And it's not merely psychological, because you can see that it's about that one being-consciousness. So the two sides coincide: the being-awareness and that direct being without any distance. That is something that many people have difficulty with because in seeing and hearing, in becoming aware, they almost always create a distance. How is non-duality ever possible there? So it's very simple: there is an internal emotional consciousness, not just in feeling, but also in feeling-seeing. In that consciousness, phenomena appear and disappear without distance. They can come; they can stay away. So with that internal consciousness there is no dependence upon phenomena. When they come there is a non-duality with the internal experience or the complete coincidence and falling away of everything. When they don't come, there is the pure being-awareness or the dissolving of everything in the Origin. Is that clear?

Spring garden
Silence:
movement
of sunspots and leaf shades,
the cooing of a dove.
Silence.

Where is time?

Light and darkness play eternally,
wind blows along my open skin.

Where am I?

One feeling is skin and wind.
As skin-wind I blow through the trees,
green skin-wind of the rustling leaves.

The utterly soft whisper has so much power
that I and everything disappear into it.

I savor the flowers' nectar;
drunk, I realize there's nothing more than: *one* taste.

Seeing is merging with glitter and shadow,
being the rapidly changing darkness and light and
their source without duality, time or place.

6.5 The body

Schiermonnikoog, July 1, 2003

The most important thing is to stay with your highest notion of Self-being, with your highest or deepest experience of Self-being. Even if this Self-being is not yet fully realized, still there is an intuitive sense of it. You can remain with that, continually. Then there is an ongoing self-meditation. The most important thing is letting that happen: staying as open as possible to your own open-being. Through this orientation the sense grows stronger and manifests increasingly in the being-experience until finally becoming a permanently aware being-experience. Then "This is it" is the full realization.

I have experienced that I'm still stuck in the body-feeling. It's just not clear to me what it means to let go of the body. I've seen people who were totally out of their bodies and walked around like zombies. And that scares me.

When I say: withdraw a few steps, I don't mean that you fly off into the air. You see and experience the whole, and you are the whole. Your body stays there as long as it's there, as well as everything else that announces itself. So internally you feel everything that you also experience. It stays exactly the same. When you truly withdraw yourself exclusively, so that you are fully situated in the highest spheres, you can certainly have difficulty returning. But, if you calmly take a few steps backwards, you are aware of yourself universally as being-awareness and you feel your bodily contact with the ground. It's not taking distance so much as it is an expansion and extension of consciousness and feeling.

So you can keep feeling that.

Of course, in the greater whole. So becoming aware as witness-consciousness is an expansion and not an escape or movement to another location at some distance.

Yes, that's why I was confused, that you would be completely gone and have no contact any longer.

Very quietly you let everything happen. You are situated in yourself, stay with yourself and experience your body. You experience an expansion when you withdraw a bit in consciousness. Then everything remains exactly the same, except that now as being-awareness you have a more spacious view because your center is no longer positioned exclusively in the body. So you're no longer tied to the bodily viewpoint, to the perspective of your bodily 'I'. The body still exists, but that existence is in space.

"Stay with yourself", do you mean that internally you also maintain bodily contact?

Certainly, the consciousness is universally open. You experience that it becomes more expansive and that the circumstances of the body don't weigh on you as heavily as they used to. Now you are so incredibly spacious. The bodily things go on as usual, but they fill just a fraction of the space that you are.

Don't you still need to care for the body?

Let your body be fully there in the great whole. Within that it receives what it needs, as a small part of the whole, that you both experience and are.

Is that what you mean by "letting go of the body"?

Exactly. Then the energies can fully develop. Of course, it's also good to experience the consciousness-sphere in a purer form, free from every form. Only, it's not necessary. The realization can also occur while you are just sitting. If you just relax you don't need to change your viewpoint. Let everything go, then your viewpoint and its attendant forms fall away. When that happens in a radical manner, something incredibly great comes in its place.

Yes, I noticed that I was always busy trying to feel my life, because I was afraid I'd fly away and become a zombie. I was really terrified of that. I didn't dare let go of the body.

There is a technique for immediately experiencing everything at the level of pure consciousness, but then, indeed, there is a danger that you cut yourself off from the world. This danger can be minimized if you stay integrated with the body, as I just explained.

Even when you turn to other levels of consciousness, bodily existence still remains. You are present there with your bodily feeling and bodily structure. For example, that's how it is when you dream. That's also the case when you envision doing a certain activity. For instance, you imagine that you will go to the beach and go swimming. Then the bodily feeling is still there. So being-experience of bodily sensations and bodily existence remain in mental situations. That's even the case on the level of the witness, because you are literally sitting and watching. That has a deep bodily component. And further: the entire field that you experience is your body. When it's cosmic, then the entire cosmos is your body. There everything is complete just as it is in your body – with an internal energetic-feeling sense and a direct comprehensive knowledge of what's going on. All energies, in so far as you experience them internally, are directly related to your bodily energies. Only now the body is open, and therefore the bodily energies coincide with other energies. Therefore the energetic self-being is everywhere. And so you can also say, "I am everything and everyone." When you emphasize consciousness too quickly, the entire middle-sphere becomes suppressed. In the Advaita tradition there is a continual push and pull between the energetic and consciousness approaches. You are pure being-awareness, free from the energies, period. But Shankara spoke in detail about energies, also about the creation of the world. With the advaita approach there can be differing emphases. For one person, one approach is suitable (you are consciousness only, nothing more) and for another, the other (you are everything). It is clear: sooner or later both approaches have to come together.

I experience my body as the center of the cosmos. Is that the distance you indicated between myself and my body?

When you see yourself as standing in the center of the cosmos, there is a duality of body-being and being-awareness. Both can truly coincide. Then the last forms dissolve and the 'situation' becomes inexpressible, because there is no 'I' and no image to describe it.

The transition from the witness towards an opening on a cosmic scale is an incredible experience. Then you dance like Shiva, then you dance the cosmos. Just let it happen. You run and dance, in and as the cosmos. Yes, it's an amazing experience. But, you just allow yourself to become increasingly relaxed therein, so that the distance between your dancing and your being-awareness can disappear. You confirm that you are as large as the whole cosmos. Then the being-awareness is an internal knowing without form. In any case, the forms are completely transparent, non-restrictive and not any different from you. It's wonderful that these kind of breakthroughs continue to come, breaking through fixed patterns. [...]

Normally we say a particular line is horizontal and therefore the sky is above it and the ground below. We sit down upon a chair, instead of hanging from the ceiling. If we did hang from the ceiling, then gravity would be directed upwards, so that everything falls up. You all have experienced this by standing on the beach for a long time with your head hanging between your knees, seeing the sandy beach as the ceiling. Then the fixed perceptual patterns were temporarily broken through. Or you play with children, so that you become free of adult patterns. That happened to someone here once, and we didn't see him for the rest of the day.

When that occurs together with an internal awareness, you can clearly confirm what it means, the liberation from fixed patterns. Everyone has had experiences that have made a large impression on them. Confirm that very precisely, so that the process of becoming free continues. When it happens in a semi- or unconscious way you can have the same beautiful experience a hundred or a thousand times, while you continue to run in little circles. Through insight into freedom, precisely on the bodily level, these circles can break open.

Everything comes from Nothing;
everything remains Nothing;
therefore everything is and remains new
and infinitely beautiful.

6.6 Freedom and pain

Good, so you are free. What are the consequences?

I don't know.

So, constrictions and limitations don't exist anymore. Can you confirm that very clearly for yourself?

Yes.

Then I hold you to it. You are free. What will you do now?

Celebrate, simply live.

Very good. And when that celebration suddenly stops. What then?

But when there is freedom that celebration doesn't stop.

Sure it does. You experience freedom as a celebration of life. Wonderful. But that stops somewhere. What then?

[Another] You can confirm that sometimes you have unpleasant feelings, so then you can say that you feel unhappy because of them.

When the peace of self-being is there, there is a great openness towards whatever presents itself, including unpleasant sensations, feelings and experiences. Whatever appears, it's not avoided. Every detail is accepted, because you are already that. So there's also a great sensitivity and compassion for the one who suffers. Even more than that: you are the other in his or her suffering.

When you talk about celebration, that it's not always necessary, I think about these sorts of things.

Certainly it's wonderful to celebrate. Only, what's it really about? When there is joy in freedom, then yes, that's a party. But that's something different than "I'll be enthusiastic about living in freedom, so I'm going to make it nice and celebrate".

Yes, exactly. For example, there can be a situation where you enjoy the nice feeling that nature brings, and you don't have that if you are in a prison. But in both situations you can experience freedom.

The real free-being remains primary. Circumstances have no influence upon it. As long as the body lives, the world of circumstances continues to exist. But then it's no longer taken in a restrictive way. First comes the One, and then the phenomena. And they are very relative.

Isn't it a mistake then to imagine that with enlightenment everything would be the same in the Self?

Phenomena are a natural part of life but they are absorbed in the great whole and are therefore relative. They arise, change and disappear once again. When you don't let yourself become obsessed and identified everything remains open and free. Then the great peace remains permanently present in the foreground. That's it.

There can still be pain.

There can be everything that can happen to the body. The advaita approach is not to get rid of the pain, but rather the victimhood.

Then it's more of a mental pain.

When there is pain, there is a physical perception of pain, just as there is a perception with the aid of the eyes.

Yes.

As long as the senses are there, they function.

So there is no longer identification with them.

We have often spoken about this. The physical things just continue normally without you being specifically involved in them. You are 'nothing' and you are everything. You walk and you don't walk. Both coincide in a way that is inexpressible. You see and you don't see from a position located specifically behind the eyes. You talk and you don't talk. We'll drink a cup of tea in a moment... and we won't drink a cup of tea. Shall we just go ahead and do that then?

6.7 Moving freely

Gouda, October 21, 2005

We have spoken about how I can be the cyclist as well as the one who perceives the cyclist. So now I can choose to be the cyclist or not.

Or both?

That's the problem.

That's what this is all about. But begin with the aspect of distance. You can perceive yourself while the cycling goes on: "I see myself cycling". You can get to know this situation better.

While you are that infinite consciousness in which you see yourself cycling, you are also internally present in that body which cycles.

You shouldn't think too much about it, or you won't come to it. It's impossible to arrive at the non-duality of different perspectives via thought.

That's exactly where I get stuck. I don't get it. I can choose...

That's precisely it. For the thinking self there is only one possibility: either you have this standpoint, or you have the other standpoint. However, the standpoints can also coincide. They can certainly be separate. You've already experienced that. Of course you can concentrate on one or you can concentrate on the other. But, when you are everything, then you experience the two standpoints simultaneously. Then there are an infinite number of standpoints, simultaneously. So there are an incredible number of perspectives, simultaneously.

But first, let's stay with these two. You can ride a bike, while you as being-awareness remain spacious. In this space you also have the situation of being there on the bike. You have a certain visual perspective there and a certain bodily feeling, which form the basis for your ability to take turns smoothly, to ride between cars, and so on. Otherwise there would be accidents.

The point is that you don't need to have your center of gravity there on that bicycle-viewpoint. The biking takes place within a greater whole, in which you participate as being-awareness. When you cycle on a quiet pathway, it goes very smoothly. You are present in the greater whole. From a distance you see yourself cycling, but also you certainly feel your body quite thoroughly from within, your feet on the pedals, your hands gripping the handlebars and your muscles pumping the pedals. You are all that too. Of course you are that. You experience it from the inside-out, just as you have always experienced living from the inside-out. The only point is that this occurs in the great whole, of which now you are also aware. And that's the difference between a fixed position on a bicycle seat. So then, it's no longer a question of the one perspective or the other. It's much more about becoming free of any specific perspective.

When you say that now it works well to view the cyclist from a distance, then you are positioned at the level of the witness. What matters then is becoming free from the viewpoint of the witness. As long as you stay situated in a particular viewpoint, even the viewpoint of the witness, there is the problem of duality: either you are positioned at the viewpoint of the witness, or the viewpoint of the cyclist.

Yes, that's the problem.

Release yourself on the level of the witness. Then you will see the conditioning of the witness.

Yes, I keep telling myself to just keep holding on there.

Turn within once again, meditatively, to yourself as witness. You are the witness of yourself as much as you are sitting there. In your consciousness you are literally positioned at a distance from that body which sits there. As your attention returns anew to yourself as witness, then what happens there?

Then you become aware of yourself on that level. You become aware of yourself as witness.

Yes, I have it very clearly now.

Stay there and then just turn around. You become aware of the whole space and you let yourself relax therein. Then there is no tension any more from the witness, no tension any more from a viewpoint.

Then there is nothing any longer, but also everything.

Precisely: non-duality. Then the cycling happens by itself. Then the witness-being happens by itself. There is no identification any more with a viewpoint. Viewpoints can certainly pop up, but they have no strength to hold you down so that you say: "I am here", or "I am there". No, everything is open.

The point is that you become aware of yourself anew. You bring your attention back to yourself, now as witness. You become aware of yourself as witness. From which viewpoint?

In any case from a more spacious 'viewpoint'. But there is

little that can be said about it.

When you become aware of yourself in the greater space and relax there, then all perspectives disappear. Where are you then? Everywhere and nowhere. Does the cycling continue? You bet, it goes on as usual. It goes on by itself, without an 'I' that is there doing something. Are you also that? Yes, of course I'm that, because I feel it all precisely from within. I'm also the witness. But not specifically, because I am everything. I can see myself from a million viewpoints. In the great whole the cycling continues by itself.

It's
normally abnormal,
impossible reality,
extremely dynamic silence,
origin continually unfolding,
unity in multiplicity:
what a wonder;
what a joy!

6.8 Spontaneous speech and action

Gouda, April 3, 2004

When I observe a subtly recurring tension, I notice that I want to do something.

It's obvious: that kind of impulse for action is better left alone as it only creates a new tension.

I experience that the dissolving and release of tensions calls for an enormous amount of energy.

It doesn't call for energy, it liberates it. The energy was restrained by tension. Tension is nothing more than trapped energy. When relaxation happens then the energy is freed.

But sometimes that energy makes me feel very restless.

When the energy is allowed to develop in space there is only relaxation. Just relax. Then it's good. Who is there to still be restless in your relaxation?

Me.

Take another look. Apparently there is still a limited 'I'-self manifesting as tension in order to maintain yourself. Within it a new unrest-tension arises through the experience that the 'I'-self is disappearing in relaxation. Take another look and experience yourself as much larger than that little 'I'. Relax anew, just let it all go.

But frequently there is an impulse to do something. And then I notice that I have reentered a restrictive situation.

I refer to phenomena on increasingly subtler levels and emphasize that the process of tension and relaxation needs to continue there. So, when tensions are present, however subtle, the thing is to recognize them anew and release them. It's an ongoing clarity and allowing that clarity to deepen itself. When the clarity isn't there, there is unrest and an impulse for restrictive action before you know it. Once again you have made a foregoing separation there between yourself and the world. So a renewed awareness and release is also necessary, a recurring expansion of awareness and release. Both can be present simultaneously and then there is a falling away of everything in clarity.

Sometimes it's necessary to do something.

Which necessity? Who should do something? In the great relaxation something certainly happens by itself. You don't need to link the impulses to an 'I'-construction.

Is a certain orientation necessary for that?

Absolutely not, precisely no orientation on anything. We have just spoken about relaxation and knowledge of that relaxation, so that it can continue infinitely. Nothing else.

But if I'm going to say something, then I'm doing something.

Yes, when there is an 'I'-do. Return again to yourself as

perceiver and experience the situation of separateness and the impulse to say something. When you're not aware of it then it's automatic. Then you have the impulse in your background, it arises in you as a limited person, and that belongs to your identity. Then you say: "I want to say something". Then there is the desire "I want to say something". Reflexively, you can turn around, previous to the impulse, and see this as a phenomenon arising in the great whole.

Then you can say finally something.

Then something is said when the speaking-energy is strong enough.

Then you are no longer the one who says something?

Then there is no 'you' or 'I' as 'speaker'. Let the expansion of awareness continue, guided by the question: where does the impulse come from?

From nowhere. The impulse is suddenly there.

Just stay there quietly observing everything. At a certain moment you see that an impulse arises. From where? Yes, from the great nothing. But, notice also when the impulse arises from something: from an 'I'-identity containing a piece of unrest, discontent or lack of clarity. The impulses "I want to say something" and "I want to do something" come from that.

When the impulses come out of nothing in the great whole, there is no "I see" and "I do". Then the processes are natural. What happens then arises spontaneously from the forces of that great whole. Just let it quietly develop. Only, stay clearly aware of the source and the great whole, because the impulse to identify yourself with the action-impulses is stubborn, quick and subtle.

Do you see how it goes back and forth:
the melting into emptiness and
the eruption into creation,
and both suddenly at once?
Inexpressible.

6.9 Morality: good conduct

Gouda, March 12, 1997

Frequently there are questions about moral action in relation to the advaita approach. Do you let go of the world? What about your behavior from an ethical point of view? In any case it's good to be aware of the moral aspects of your existence.

Moral rules

When see your own actions and the actions of others, you often have a moral judgment about it. When a strong fellow attacks another one who is weak, and for no good reason, you naturally empathize with the weaker one and have a strong feeling or belief that such behavior shouldn't be allowed. Reference is often made to general rules or laws in order to answer the question of why it shouldn't be allowed. Thus action is frequently associated with moral criteria. The call for morality in our society is steadily increasing: people should be observing moral rules more often, no corruption, no vandalism, no large public nuisance, and so on. So besides the pure moral rules which people are called upon to observe, there are also rules which are fixed into law and regulations which are maintained by the police. Additionally, there are some less stringent rules which are useful for achieving something: for example, when you want to follow a spiritual path, you try to behave in such and such a way. In the Classical Yoga of Patañjali, *yama* and *niyama* are described as the first steps along the eightfold path with prescriptions about what you must and must not do. Moral rules have a certain force. Though they may not be fixed within the laws of the state, in society they are followed more or less.

Are the rules still so compelling these days? Frequently yes, but especially so in a forceful situation where there's the sense that morality isn't really about fixed rules, after all. What is it based on, then? A fundamental feeling which lies beneath, or as it is often said, on an insight into good conduct and a good selection of rules. We need to look into this more precisely.

The moral feeling and the moral being

Morality as moral feeling appears especially connected with co-feeling or sym-pathy. Nobody lives physically-emotionally isolated within his or her skin. The emotional and energetic body extends itself far out into the world. The intensity of the feeling-energy decreases with distance, but nowhere is there an absolute end to it. In principal it extends on into infinity.

Usually people limit their sympathy to their immediate surroundings and often only a few people with whom they choose to be close to. In everyday life the feeling or heart energies are, for the most part, firmly contained within an 'I'-core (ego). This ego is nothing other than a chunk of energy concentrated into a point. In spiritual development, the ego can also play a role and then people are inclined to put their moral sense on the backburner. Everyone already has their hands full with themselves. The other is certainly important, but what is one's own comes first, one's individual life.

Nevertheless, sooner or later you open up emotionally. You become open and you relax. Which is to say that you become more sensitive to what presents itself to you, you don't push things away so forcibly. This means that your feeling-body spreads outwards in all directions. You flow outwards into the sphere of others. That is love towards others. You don't hold your self-being fixed in a center, but are decentralized, streaming into other living beings. Your self-being ultimately coincides with the self-being of others. You are the self of the other. You see yourself in everything and everything in yourself. In the Ishā Upanishad 6 it states:

He who perceives all beings
in the Self alone,

and the Self in all beings,
does not entertain any hatred on account of that perception.

In 6.29 of the Bhagavadgītā it is written:

He whose self has become whole through yoga,
sees himself in all beings,
And all beings in himself…

Isn't that the full honor and meaning of the second great commandment of Christianity: "Thou shalt love thy neighbor as thyself" (Matthew 22:39)? That kind of love isn't possible in a duality, when you stand apart from the other: "I am me and the other is the other". That love is possible only when you recognize your self as the self of the other. Then love is a simply a matter of course. Yājñavalkya says: "It is not for the sake of the man that the man is lovable, but he is loveable for the sake of the Âtman; it is not for the sake of the wife that the wife is loved, but she is loved for the sake of the Âtman," and so on (Brhadāranyaka Upanishad 4.5.6). Love is not a thing that you can give; it is the sphere that arises in which there is no separation any more between your own self-being and the self of another. Then the duality has transformed into a non-duality (a-dvaita).

In this sense, spiritual development and the strengthening of the moral sense go hand in hand. It becomes increasingly clear that the comm-unity sphere is always already present. The symbiotic relationship of the child to its mother precedes the creation of a separate individual. It follows quite naturally and understandably that people, prior to the development of the thinking function, know what it's like for another being to enjoy and to suffer, that there is sympathy for each other, that people have understanding for each other, that they have pity and compassion, that they display moral behavior. Moral behavior has its foundation in the non-duality of I and thou.

Moral insight and consciousness

There is also a second foundation of morality. Often the intellectual understanding of the necessity of moral rules is seen as the source of moral behavior. A community of people with a certain amount of self-centeredness won't function without rules that organize living together to some degree. We want to be as free as possible in our lives; but in order not to restrict the freedom of others too much, we all have to restrict our own freedom a little bit. In principle all social and religious rules and laws are issued to create a better life and society. Recognizing the reasonable aspect of moral rules is the rational basis for following them. This occurs from an independent and rational 'I' that, in principle, is free of rules. The person alone decides to follow, or not to follow, rules from their own insight.

But this rational and reasonable 'I' clearly has 'I'-structures, the most important of which is self-centeredness, through which the separation between 'I' and not-'I' is made. So, this 'I' has its own self-interest and when that 'I' feels itself to be completely free in its actions, this self-interest plays a role in its behavior. Behavior that harms others is all too frequently condoned from self-interest. Certain excuses are always offered: "Don't others do it too?" "It isn't so bad, is it?" Thus, moral freedom doesn't really exist, as long as there is an 'I'. When the 'I' has completely disappeared, there is no self-interest any longer. But what does that mean, that there is no 'I' anymore? In the direction of the 'I' as increasingly purified consciousness, an 'I'-quality always remains, as long as there is something.

Societal rules are externally imposed precisely because the 'I'-know revolves around self-centeredness and you are required to be responsible for your own actions. Traditionally it was the father-figure who, with a piercing glance, saw to what extent self-interest had caused harm to be done to others, who saw to what extent the law had been violated. In Judaism and Christianity it is God who determines the law and judges people accordingly; whether they have lived in compliance with that law or not. In relation to other people, there are also those who are entitled to receive help and there are victims who with just their glance proclaim all the law of moral behavior. But what's that really about? About a higher consciousness which brings the limitations of the ego into the light, illuminating the self-interest that harms others and increases suffering. Ultimately that consciousness is the clarity of the great openness in which there is no 'I' who can grasp onto itself any longer.

That clarity is also to be discovered within yourself. From that clarity you know what is good and what is bad. It is your 'conscience' which recognizes that everything which restricts is wrong and everything that expands is good. Conscience allows you to see that you are not confined by the limiting 'I'-characteristics. This happens on a spiritual path. Then there is a purification, which is to say that the 'I' becomes more rarified, but also takes on increasingly cosmic dimensions. And with that internal expansion it also becomes more connected to everything. So, all that is said about the outflow of sympathy in morality still applies here. This feeling becomes universal and this universal sensitivity, along with the release of the 'I', frees you from the limitations of the 'I'-feeling. Here on the path of insight, both spiritual development and the strengthening of morality go hand in hand.

The non-duality

Thus, we saw that morality is most complete when the limited 'I' has disappeared and a universal sensitive-being exists. This maximum morality exists at the edge of Nothing, where the 'I' is swept away and forgotten through the functioning of the Nothing, the Clarity. This Clarity pushes the Law of the disappearance of the 'I' on through and with it liberates the self-being to recognize that original unity feeling with everything and everyone. To the extent that there is still an action, it is extremely moral and takes place spontaneously without an 'I'. Fortunately, there are situations in your own experience in which this has already happened and so it's good for you to recognize that. There are situations in which you helped someone in need, helped without constraint from moral rules, without first getting advice about your own feelings and without needing to check the correctness of helping in that particular situation. When people ask why you helped, you answer that 'of course' you helped. There's no reason to give. Afterwards you can say that you must have felt your connection with the other and that you acted in accordance with moral precepts. But that's a conclusion made afterwards. In the situation of total help there was no 'I', because there was only an event in relation to someone else. Was a law imposed externally? A glance from an Other that you couldn't avoid? No, because in most cases you conclude this after the fact. In the situation itself there was a forgetting of the 'I', of divisions, of conduct. There was nothing. Yet there was a complete accordance with moral precepts and a total empathy and insight apparently present. It is precisely through the absence of an 'I' that there is this totality of the different aspects of morality. On the one hand, the 'I' is Nothing, and on the other hand, complete-being. In non-duality these co-exist, without the contradictions that occur in the thought process. This non-dual coincidence of Not-being and the complete spontaneous morality of All-being is the highest wisdom.

It's always new and miraculous,
the emergence of things and the waves of events,
while nothing happens
in the quiet simplicity.

6.10 Everything continues, frictionless

Schiermonnikoog, June 2000

Everyone here can point to their greatest experiences. Now I want to especially point out something a little less obvious. In the break when we stopped with our yoga, there was some tea, there was some conversation, some movement, but the whole situation remained quiet, clear and frictionless.

There is speech, but there is also silence in and around the conversation. There are movements, but there is also motionlessness. There is a mutual communication, but there is no clash, no action and reaction. There is *communion*, togetherness, unity. When you are alert, you notice it. Then you also see the difference between this and another situation in which there is the duality of 'I'-persons. Through comparison you can see great differences. And suddenly there it is, an inexpressible peace. Conversation continues normally, tea drinking continues normally, a few carry on with the yoga movements, others are sitting quietly. It is deeply touching. See it, recognize it, through recognition it can also continue. Once again, always, the clarity, the insight: "this is it". What is the quality of that situation?

We do energetic exercises together. There is a back and forth flow of energy, but that flow is frictionless, spontaneous, creative, perfect. It's good to confirm this quality quite explicitly. It also has the quality of being-one, because divisions between people aren't there. No one defends his own position and territory against anyone else. In conversations there is a lot more than just mutual recognition; there is joint recognition of the profound unity that already always existed. The energies continue on in a greater whole, without conflicts, without grasping onto anything, without solidifying anywhere. It's a merging in the stream of a greater togetherness. It's worthwhile recognizing this.

While the movements take place spontaneously and the

conversations go on in a normal way, the unity remains. When you are alert, you clearly confirm that the diversity within the unity is wonderful. You have to see what a beautiful collection of people are walking around here, yourself included. Isn't that wonderful? There is a savoring of the wealth. It's touching to see each other. That emotion becomes infinite, and in that rudderless expanse you lose your last foothold. That is love: to cherish each other so much that you coincide with one another. That's more than devotion.

And the energies continue, without clinging to anything, without resisting anything, without there being an 'I' who resists something. Then the energies are very expansive and creative. Fountains of energy spraying up and splashing back down. The spinning circles are beautiful. It's a magnificent game, a wonderful collective game, the collective dance that forms spontaneously, without technique. Everything happens in the whole. The energies flow in incredible colors, beautiful shapes, in complete accord.

See it. Only through insight does it stabilize. This is it. You know that. You recognize the situation.

I began the first night by saying: you are free. You should take a look sometime at what processes were at work to have fully recognized that. Again and again there were breakthroughs in those firmly built structures. Again there was a melting of those structures, the melting away of what was initially held so strongly by the ego-forces. It was a momentous occasion for everyone, for some to a very high degree. Apparently the time is ripe for it. When the seed of the dandelion is ripe, the wind just takes the seeds away with it. You can't predict when that will happen. You can only say: a particular ripeness is needed. Suddenly there is a cloud of flying seeds. They are loose, because they don't cling to the receptacle of the plant anymore. Ripe apples just fall. No scientist can predict exactly when the apples will fall.

But you shook the tree really hard!

If the apples don't fall, nothing happens. What happens to the apples that ripen but don't let go?

They rot.

Exactly. And they shrivel, while remaining stuck to the tree. When the apples are ripe, it's time for them to fall. The same is true for the dandelion seeds. When it's time, they go with the wind. Then the energies can continue to flow. It's a natural process.

From the standpoint of clarity, remaining fixed is also an event that takes place in the entirety of the processes. In the creation, energies are not the same everywhere. So there is even an acceptance of the 'I'-tension and the duality that remains present in all different kinds of places. You see that the tension causes suffering and that's unfortunate. Only through awareness can the tension and suffering disappear.

Life goes on as long as it goes on. The talking continues, the drinking of tea, the moving, everything in a totally free manner in the big picture, without friction, without clashing, without conflict. Everything has, through the absence of boundaries, an infinite dimension in itself. And this dimension goes forth into the inexpressible. Everything exists and lives from there. Beauty comes from there. You are That. Then there is an inexpressible sphere of consciousness-joy-being.

Brahman is not this and not that.
Brahman is the self of everything.
It is the self of me.
Even I am the self of everything:
Even I am not this and not that.

7

The being-experience of non-duality

Non-duality can be known, not as an objective state, but rather as a sphere in which yourself and the other coincide without difficulty. The experience of non-duality then is a first-person being-experience that is internal, inclusive, direct and certain.

7.1 Confirming for yourself

Gouda, November 12, 2007

The most difficult point on the advaita path isn't so much about experiencing something special, but it's much more about trusting your own experience, confirming for yourself what manifests. Everyone will have to determine how it is with themselves and with their experienced reality, experimentally, through observation. When you see something plainly, you confirm: that's how it is. For example, the world is not stable, but comes in fragments now and then. This also applies to your body. Often the body isn't there and hardly ever as depicted in anatomy books. Images of yourself are there only now and then. When you don't specifically think about it there is no limited self-being. Apparently you must confirm something extremely clearly in order to accept what your experience brings and to use that as a decisive argument against all the stories that others have told you, that you've taken on and that you've told yourself: this is me, with these forms, with this body, with this name and so on… Be extremely clear and take your own experience seriously. Be honest with it. Then you conclude: that's how it is.

Sometimes others say: "You are busy with such vague things and are acting on faith." It's clear: it's not about faith and it's precisely not about vague things. What things are vague? Those are the things that people, individually and collectively, have constructed in their heads: ideas, images, recollections, dreams, expectations, prejudices. They are just creations, yet they certainly determine people's reality. They are limited forms into which everything is molded. Go back to your own experience, throw it open, examine things for yourself and confirm: this is how it is and not otherwise. Go back to your own experience.

7.2 Experiencing self-being

In Advaita Post Vol. 7 Number 15 (September 19, 2006)

What is self-being? Self-being as an aware being-experience doesn't appear to be obvious to everyone. This is caused in part by a strong focus on external things. Then you forget yourself as the source of that focus. This lack of direct experience comes partly through a neglect of the body. In advaita circles self-being is often taken to be nothing more than consciousness (mental or supra-mental), but due to the extreme subtlety of that consciousness it is only clearly experienced with great sensitivity. For many then, consciousness remains a mental abstraction. In order to allow self-experience to be perceptible practically, it's good to return to the experience of self-being as it manifests every day. In daily life, there is a clear concretely perceptible bodily sphere of self-being.

Everyone has a sense of I, myself, and that 'myself' is, above all, a bodily self. Usually there is a looking and acting from an 'I' in the body. Thus, 'I' am located in the bodily sphere. 'I' am identified with this sphere.

What does this bodily sphere look like? In order to determine this, attention must no longer be focused outwards on external things, but brought back to your inner physical space. It's good to do that very concretely by slowly bringing the point of attention back towards yourself. That point of attention then comes inside the body via the skin. What do you experience then within the bodily sphere?

Primarily, there are bodily impressions and feelings. To the extent that you don't take a distance from them, they have an 'I'-quality. It is your own inner sphere, distinct from the external world. You experience these impressions and feelings quite clearly. In this situation that is a concrete experience of self-being.

The bodily impressions and feelings take up a certain space. Therefore they are spatial energies that tingle, pulsate, radiate, sometimes with a pressure. Notice how easily these feeling energies are trapped by the forms that your mind creates, the familiar forms of your body. The mental forms then ensure that the bodily energies do not go their own way. To the extent that you are identified with the body, you close yourself off in this form. Fortunately, the cognitive forms can fall away. This happens when you relax. In relaxation you sink into the feeling-body and you experience yourself in an open, sensitive way. What do you experience then?

Your feeling energies appear to expand unhindered. Just go into it: how far do the energies/the feelings radiate to the right? Go with them to the right. Can you discover a border anywhere? You are infinitely expanded to the right in your bodily feeling. This applies to all directions, to the left, forwards and backwards, above and below: you are infinitely large, as large as the entire cosmos.

With every expansion, your own self-being continues to retain the quality of your bodily starting point. With the initial expansion, a short distance from the physical body, the physical quality is still quite strong. When you stay with it, remaining concretely aware with a great presence of mind, you also experience that same quality of self in cases of greater expansion. That quality is always more rarefied, but the concrete experience of self-being remains. Then as a being-experience it is obvious: I have no limits; I am as spacious as the entire cosmos. Of course you are the physical body, too, but that needn't imprison you. You are everything. In everything, in all things, in all living beings, the concrete individual self-quality exists: there is universal self-being. Within that everything is no longer experienced at a distance through observation, but from within, from the self-being of everything and everyone.

This self-being also has the aspect of consciousness that has a quality of non-being. This already applies on the level of the every day body. You are that body, but you confirm from your consciousness that you don't fully coincide with it. This going hand in hand of first and third person is present on all levels of self-being. By taking distance on the level of the witness consciousness, a physicality is still present, which has few properties it's true, but nevertheless you know and are that. In that self-experience a physicality remains which coincides with a more spacious consciousness. This greater space of consciousness is the foundation for the transition towards a release of the last viewpoint and the cosmic expansion. Then once again there is a body, which now coincides with the whole cosmos. There *is* nothing else, except a higher consciousness in which it is affirmed that everything becomes more rarefied and can disappear into that which is absolute. Up until the last, being and non-being go together in an inimitable way as non-dual being-awareness. Immeasurable joy and love also arise in this non-duality. This non-dual self-being remains in the foreground as totally self-evident, as long as there is anything.

7.3 Inclusive experience

In: Advaita Post 6 Number 15 (September 5, 2005)

Limitation of your own world and yourself occurs on all different levels of functioning, not only on the level of thought but on the level of sense experience, too. Seeing something that interests you all too quickly becomes a concentration, whereby the visual field becomes narrowed to the object and you become reduced to the seer of exclusively that object. This means that the object becomes detached from the environment and that you limit yourself to a distant point of observation with an exclusive (visual) connection to the observed. From that perspective, the pulling-one-thing-out-from-the-other (analysis) easily proceeds. Parts are differentiated and segregated. Scientists do this to an extreme degree, beginning from the smallest particles in the hopes of being able to understand everything.

This objectification with its analytical approach has its utility. However, the negative consequences of its societal expression have become very clear in both the separation of people from their environment and in their disproportionate expression of individualism. Attempts to form a synthesis from fragments appear to be difficult and hardly ever succeed. Another approach is truly possible. It is found more often in non-Western cultures than in our own. In the August 27, 2005 edition of *New Scientist* there was an article about an experiment in which the eye movements of students were recorded as they were looking at images of a figure against a background. One image included a tiger in a jungle. American students looked much longer at the figure than the Chinese students did, who saw the figure but whose visual perception also included the background. Apparently, so the researchers concluded, westernized East Asians have more attention for the context of phenomena than Western people do. This context includes not only the visual field before you, but also your own feeling being-awareness.

During the retreat on Schiermonnikoog we do different exercises for the inclusive experience. The next exercise is, in essence, as follows.

Expansion of your feeling energy

Stand with your face towards the sea. Look at the point of the horizon before you. Feel your feet and hands. Let the feeling energy go outwards from your feet and your hands over the beach and the sea, while your hands go upwards to the height of the horizon. With your hands and your feeling body feel the sand and the water. You flow out like an amoeba to the point on the horizon before you. Continue experiencing the entire space before you as your own body…

Then go with your right hand, with your gaze and your feeling, to the right along the horizon and over the sea and also let yourself expand. Keep looking at the horizon, but experience the space in between as yourself, up to a 90° section of a circle. Do the same to the left. Do the same with steps to the left then the right, continuing around, until you feel aware of the whole circle of the horizon and you are that flat circular disk. Experience yourself physically, from within and from without, as both the center of the circle and the entire circular disk. You are the horizon, you are everywhere. There are no separations. There is no duality.

Through this experiment there is a breaking open of the experience-schema of the body, 'I' and world, a recognition of your own open being-awareness. As open being-awareness you are the broad context in which everything that appears has a place.

So, physically you can become completely free, you can become so spacious that your physicality coincides with the cosmos. The cosmos then is the bodily organism in which everything is related to everything else. It remains as your body; therefore you are the entire cosmos, as first person. Because you are internally present everywhere, the cosmos has a 'field-character' in which you directly experience everything. The internal sensitivity is everywhere. Therefore you affirm everything directly, just as in everyday life when you immediately know where a mosquito has bitten you and where it hurts. Through that there is always a coincidence of the external perspective "I see my body there" and the internal perspective "I experience myself as body from inside out". They go together seamlessly just as the perspectives from your two eyes seamlessly coincide in the view from a set of binoculars. They come together and deliver something new to the experience of seeing: the depth of the world. There is a problem-free merging of the internal and external experience and an arising of something new: the depth of the non-duality.

7.4 Direct confirmation

Heerenveen, October 20, 2001

Knowledge of yourself is very different from the knowledge of things. When you see a chair, you see it there at a distance as an object. That can also be the case for your own bodily and mental affairs. You can take distance from them too, so that you observe them as objects. In so far as you experience your body as object you can disassemble it and if needed even cut into it. Additionally, there is an internal knowledge of your body and your mind. You know yourself not so much as object, but rather internally in the sphere of yourself. That is a completely different sort of knowledge than object-knowledge. When you do all kinds of things, the body is not an object. Even when you view your body as an instrument of action, it has a first-person character. So you also have an internal knowledge of it. When it comes to self-knowledge, there is an internal knowing in which there is no distance between subject and object. You yourself are both subject and object. Therefore the knowing is direct. When a mosquito bites you, you immediately know exactly where that has happened. When you have pain in your knee, you immediately know that you have pain in your knee. If the doctor says: "You can't be having any pain because there's nothing wrong with your knee," still you know, when it hurts, it hurts. You confirm it internally right away and this direct internal confirmation can't be refuted by anyone. For this there is no other authority than yourself. It forms the greatest truth that there is. Of course afterwards you can certainly form other conclusions, when you have new experiences and gain new insights. But even then you experience everything once again in a direct manner. The hallmark of self-knowledge is that it is a direct knowing, without distance and intermediary, internal and unquestionable.

In everyday perception it can also happen that an object comes so close that it's really going to coincide with you. Then there is absolutely nothing more. In any case you can't say anything about it. Subject and object have come together. When you remain very aware there is still a subject quality, but the object has been absorbed within it. There is no difference anymore. You can't even say that it is a positive unity. You can only say: there is no difference any more between subject and object, there is a non-duality. Try it out.

Subject and object coming together

Bring one hand up to eye level before you and look at it. Then you see the shape, surface structure and color. It is an object that you can see externally. Then let your hand come closer to your face. What happens? Now you need to remain very alert because you take distance all too easily and create a beautiful projected image of yourself with your hand, or conversely you stay at the position of your eyes looking out. No, stay very clearly focused on your hand and experience what there is to experience as your hand comes closer to your face. You can repeat this with a ballpoint pen or another object of your choice.

When you remain aware of yourself (subject) and your hand (object) and both truly come together, then the hand disappears and you also disappear. Everything is gone. And you confirm it too. How is that possible? In the blank state there is still a knowing! Even if everything doesn't disappear, there is a realm that can't be described, because subject and object run through one another. That's the case with the self-experience of your body. Your hand then has both subjective as well as objective aspects. When you become aware of something, both are already separated out. First there is the experience that something is there. Later you experience that it is a hand. Both types of experience concern the being-there of something and these experiences are direct. You confirm that being-there directly or you don't. Only through further differentiation, the divergence of subject and object, do the conceptual determinations of thinking arise which mediate perception.

These sorts of simple experiences, which occur quite often and that everyone actually knows, tip the balance towards becoming free. You'll just need to confirm it very cleary. In principle, everyone knows the coincidence of subject and object. Everybody knows themselves as an infinitely deep dimension that is not objectifiable. You'll just have to confirm it clearly for yourself.

Everything we discuss concerns your own experience, your own being-experience, and so it's about your own direct confirmation. Don't start thinking, because the 'I'-think works indirectly, with images as tools, with old mental constructs. In the direct experience everything is open, everything is always new.

What function does memory have then?

Memory is a mental construct, too. Have you ever seen a memory? Is it a bin from which you withdraw pictures? When you go home, there is an event in the great whole and that just happens, so to speak. And it goes on in an adequate way, because you reach your home. The knowledge is there, apparently. Anything else you say about it, for instance that there are memory-images which help you to orient yourself, is a mental construction. When there is knowledge of a reality, it's just there, irreducible.

The brain certainly has something to do with it.

You see the brain, when the skull-cap is lifted. It's only real from a certain perspective. But there are other perspectives from which it is irrelevant. When you perform your martial arts does your brain have anything to do with it? When you stand there before the other, you stand there with no past, without brains and without memory. When you do have them, you lose your presence of mind and get tossed down. Also in daily life you hardly ever have brains. When you're talking with someone, do you create any images of yours or his brain? So see the relativity of these mental constructs and don't keep hanging around in them. You can release everything you have learned. At a certain point in spiritual development it's no longer important. What is truly important? Your own being-sphere. When you return there with attention there is a direct intuitive knowing. The standard knowing is always indirect because it uses intermediaries. You use your senses: your eyes, your ears; you use your memory. You use these as means to come to a certain knowledge and further experience. If these intermediaries should once all fall away, the object of knowledge would coincide with yourself. You have already had that in your own being experience.

Keep your presence of mind aligned with your own experience and everything will become clear to you. The depth of the non-duality with everything and everyone is directly situated within your own self-being being-awareness. When you experience this as inalienably your own, nothing else needs to happen.

7.5 Knowledge of the original state

Stoutenburg, August 28, 2005

You point towards the open clarity, even in dreamless sleep. I understand very well what you mean, but when you go to sleep you disappear. When you wake up again, there is a sort of recollection of the openness. Some people claim that when they sleep they can retain the lucid openness. Is that really so?

When you have consciously recognized the original openness somewhere, you recognize that sphere more easily and more frequently. In the waking period of the day you recognize more and more of those quiet moments, even though they were previously there. When the recognition is there in a given situation, such as in deep meditation, the process of recognition goes further, especially during the day. Then you notice the moments when it is totally still and totally open, moments about which there's nothing to say because there is no content. Between thoughts everything falls silent. Thought flow is not continuous. Also, you aren't always busy. When you don't have anything to do for a few moments, everything falls away. Slowly you recognize that these periods come more often and become larger. It happens just like a Swiss cheese: the holes just keep getting bigger. At first there is cheese with a few holes. At a certain point there are holes with a bit of cheese. All this happens by itself at night.

Of course it's a completely different kind of consciousness. It's not a consciousness of something. That's how it's usually defined in the West. When there's nothing, it's difficult to recognize. So if you want to be very aware of something, you ask right away where you need to look. When it's about the recognition of your own openness, it's a totally different type of consciousness. It is an internal consciousness and certainly without content. It is very strange and therefore you frequently make mistakes. You want to be aware of the dreamless sleep where nothing is. And so you say, "I will focus on nothing." But then that's wrong, because there is no object, also no empty object-space that you can become aware of. Then you remain looking at an empty place. No, it's not an object; it's not a direct object, the 'that' in the expression "I see that". It's your own being-awareness of yourself as first person.

It's a blank being-knowledge without a someone that confirms something.

How is it then? Isn't there then a kind of conscious presence?

You are going in the right direction when you suggest "a conscious presence". However, be careful and notice what else is there. As long as there is a notion of "I confirm that", you're still functioning with an 'I' and an object. The best approach is to point towards the falling away of the structure "I perceive that": 'I' gone, 'that' gone and the perceiving gone. That is the original blank state about which you can't say anything other than: "it is blank", "there is nothing". And yet there is an internal knowledge of this original nature.

But then, isn't it a remembrance afterwards?

Of course not. If it were a memory, there would be a memory-image. Now, that can also be true, such as in the morning when you say: "I slept very well last night" and then create a memory image of the delightful state of emptiness in which there was nothing. But the remembrance can also be so strong in the moment, that you recognize that the 'state' is also here now. It's not something that stops with the transition from the dreamless sleep to dreaming and then waking. No, it remains there all the time as a certain kind of concurrent knowing, a being-knowing. This proceeds by itself and intensifies.

This being-knowing has nothing to do with concepts and words. The empty being-experience and even further the non-dualistic experience can't be put into words. There is no description possible for emptiness and the coincidence of subject and object. So you shouldn't listen to the words of the teacher. Then the object-character of the words that were spoken falls away and you recognize something of the truth which can't be objectified in words. Then there is a coincidence of the word and its meaning, of the teacher, of the sphere towards which he points, and yourself. Then there is insight. So remain with your precise seeing, your recognizing, including that of the pure non-dual sphere.

In that blank consciousness, the 'consciousness of something' also manifests.

Yes, 'consciousness of' something is always a limited sort of consciousness. Usually we call that 'attention'. Attention is a focused consciousness and therefore a limited form of consciousness. So there are all different kinds of consciousness-forms during the day. Sometimes you concentrate here, and then something else demands your attention, and then there is a more spacious consciousness. It goes on all by itself. The only thing that remains is you as open being-awareness.

With a 'consciousness of' are you the same as that which is seen?

When there is a clear recognition of your being-awareness without restrictions, all forms come up within it without restricting you. That also applies to all vital functions such as seeing, feeling, hearing, thinking and so forth. They also come free when there is a recognition of the original. With enlightenment all life functions become enlightened. With it, the tensions disappear, the feeling patterns of grasping. When your being-awareness comes free, external things also come free. When you remain positioned within a limited identity, you hold not only yourself imprisoned, but the world, too. When enlightenment breaks through, the whole world becomes enlightened. Nothing needs to go away; you are everything. Only the tension-restrictions fall away. Then everything is open, infinitely open. Then every single thing is a miracle: how is it that it exists? And it remains a miracle, because it's not framed in thought-forms.

While there are phenomena, the openness remains. You are that openness and you are the phenomena. Subject and object coincide in an inexpressible reality. When there are no phenomena, the openness remains. The pure Âtman-Brahman is without qualities, nothing. Here too, there is nothing that can be said. Still, there is a rarefied being-knowing of the merging of yourself in the Absolute, being in non-being.

Such an experience is also there in the creation of the cosmos. The first undifferentiated space arose, the unlimited being and consciousness. All things and events come from this non-duality in a process of differentiation. Dualities arise everywhere. It is clear that everything has non-duality as its foundation. This is especially clear in areas where the separation is not fully complete, such as in communication and moral conduct. Non-duality remains as a pre-condition for the possibility of understanding one another, for empathy and giving help to others. In and through these phenomena the sun of the non-dual shines. People bask in it. And, you are that sun.

7.6 The certainty of the confirmation

Hoorneboeg, April 3, 2004

It's very beautiful that we share the advaita-insight with each other, because otherwise I might think that it's something I've just pulled out of my head.

Of course it can be wonderful to realize that there is a great inter-subjectivity in affirming the non-dual nature of self and reality. That's also true. But don't make the community too important. Many communal visions are mass illusions. No, affirm for yourself internally when more space comes and confirm also that this expansion has more value than the limited personal world. So you confirm the truth for yourself, free of others, direct in your own being-experience, very aware, with the maximum possible presence of mind. That is crucial.

But can you verify your own experience for yourself?

Already and almost always you verify what you experience quite immediately, while you experience it, not through other things or other people. With only a few exceptions is there doubt. That's how it goes in ordinary life. If, as a scientist, you discover something new, of course you should test it against what others say and have found; it should also be confirmed by others. But here it's not about something that requires an outside confirmation. No, it's immediately, internally clear, just like pain in your body. You confirm it directly without distance and without intermediaries. The direct conscious realization is the only thing that counts. What has value in your life? You can only confirm directly for yourself, not indirectly. When you leave this confirmation to others, then you remain dependent, like an uncritical follower. Then you remain uncertain. This uncertainty only moves to certitude when the internal and immediate confirmation comes: for me, this is the most important.

See the transition from dream to waking. Inherent in being awake is the knowledge: this is a higher realm of consciousness; this is a higher form of reality than the dream reality. "Fortunately, that villain who was chasing me was just a dream." You don't have to say anything more about it.

When you are fully awake and confirm the truth on the level of the highest and most spacious insight, there is absolutely no doubt any longer.

But if you don't cherish that, it quickly disappears.

It's not a matter of cherishing, but of staying internally alert. In the great clarity it's affirmed: "that's how it is". Then it simply remains as self-evident. You don't have to do anything about it.

Should I replace the word 'cherish' with 'find valuable'?

That is still far too dualistic: "I find something else valuable". Sometime later there will be something else that you find valuable. When something becomes clear with the greatest possible lucidity, you are so involved with it that it unquestionably becomes your own clear truth of existence. When someone who has spent his entire life in prison is suddenly released, he might perhaps in the beginning say: "I can't believe it; I must have a confirmation that I'm really free." But, he will also confirm it directly for himself when he leaves the prison and begins to run around outside.

Every day we crawl back into that prison, because we believe in it.

Until you have seen through that illusion and have had enough of it. Then you say: "For me it's clear; it's no longer necessary." Be independent in your confirmation: this is it. Then there is no doubt anymore, no more searching, then no confirmation is needed.

Is there really no choice? The final realization – is it completely out of your hands?

No. If I still say something about it, it's only to let something break loose in you in the sphere of your feelings and insight. Maybe then you will be able to awaken totally relaxed. In complete relaxation you confirm for yourself that your true nature coincides with the groundless source and foundation.

References

The Advaita Center

The activities of the Openness Foundation are gathered together in the Advaita Center in Gouda, the Netherlands. The Advaita Center focuses on developing education and research activities and services for the areas of life and living where insight into non-duality plays a main role. The Center is expressly interested in dialogue with other spiritual/philosophical currents.

September through May, Douwe offers weekly satsangs, weekends, week-long retreats and instruction focused on existential insight into the absence of duality (advaita). Research and practical education are organized through the study and practice departments. There are project groups organized for non-dual philosophy, psychotherapy/psychiatry, management, prose/poetry and youth. There are also courses in meditation, hatha yoga, chakra yoga and pranayama: all with a focus on non-duality.

The Internet

News and regular teaching texts are available via the free bi-weekly e-zine 'Advaita Post'. You can sign up to receive the Advaita Post via Douwe's English language blog site: http://thegroundlessopenness.wordpress.com/. Also, additional English language information about Douwe and the Advaita Center is available from the Advaita Center's main website: http://www.advaitacentrum.nl/en.

MANTRA
BOOKS

9781780992891